IS IT TRUE WHAT THEY SAY ABOUT DIXIE?

IS IT TRUE
WHAT THEY SAY
ABOUT DIXIE?

by Dian Eaton

CITADEL PRESS

Secaucus, New Jersey

Published by Citadel Press
A division of Lyle Stuart, Inc.
120 Enterprise Ave., Secaucus, N.J. 07094
A division of General Publishing Co. Limited
Don Mills, Ontario

Queries regarding rights and permissions should be
addressed to Lyle Stuart, 120 Enterprise Ave.,
Secaucus, N.J. 07094

Manufactured in the United States of America

Library of Congress Cataloging-in-Publication Data

Eaton, Dian.
     Is it true what they say about Dixie? / by Dian Eaton.
        p.   cm.
     Bibliography: p.
     ISBN 0-8065-1104-4 : $7.95
     1. English language--Provincialisms--Southern States--Glossaries,
vocabularies, etc. 2. Americanisms--Southern States--Glossaries,
vocabularies, etc. 3. Southern States--Popular culture--Miscellanea. I. Title.
PE2926.E18   1988
427'.975--dc 19   88-19753
                                                                       CIP

CONTENTS

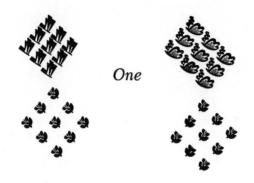

One

DIXIELAND

AWAY DOWN SOUTH IN DIXIE, on the other side of the
Mason-Dixon Line, live a colorful, romantic and pride-
ful people, the Southerners. The South was the only
country in modern history to start a war without a single cannon factory. Was this Southern pride, Southern
stupidity or Southern naivete? Probably all of these.

The Mason-Dixon Line was a boundary surveyed by
two English astronomers, Charles Mason and Jeremiah
Dixon, in the 1760's. Originally, this line separated
Pennsylvania and Maryland, but in 1779 was extended
westward to become the boundary between West Virginia and Pennsylvania. The Mason-Dixon Line became
thought of as the boundary between the North and the
South, the free and the slave states.

2

The South is that great body of land below the Mason-Dixon Line, extending westward through Southern Indiana, Southern Illinois, most of Missouri, Kansas, Oklahoma, Texas and all the remaining states eastward.

The Southern population has grown by natural increase rather than by the waves of immigration that swept the more industrial North. Therefore, the same principal population divisions as the original settlers have pretty well been maintained: the Anglo-Saxons, the Scotch-Irish, the Germans, French, Spanish, Mexicans, and the Africans.

The typical Southerner is very proud of his Southern heritage and has a traditionally long memory. It is said that the Southerner is still fighting the Civil War, or, as he prefers to call it, the War Between the States. He may appear to be easygoing and inclined toward laziness, but he is quick to speak his mind to defend his beliefs, his country and his family.

Southerners have a strong code of honor, a strong sense of moral and religious standards, and a strong sense of family. The South is extremely clannish. Everyone knows his place and most keep to it. Customs die hard here. The "old families" are very much revered. Life in the South, in general, is like life in any small town, where everyone knows everyone else and everyone's else's business, kinfolk, likes, dislikes, and idiosyncracies.

Southerners are not always as simple as they look and never as simple as they talk. On the whole, Southerners are a contradiction. They may be emotionally violent yet lazy, educated yet illogical, genteel yet ruthless. It is said that the men of the pre-Civil War South were gentlemen with genteel manners who made a business of pleasure while their Yankee compatriots made a pleasure of business.

The lower-class Southerner, however, is considered to be shiftless, illiterate and quick to show violence. He is a "redneck," a "hellraiser" or, worse, "po' white trash." This, of course, is an exaggeration, but this extreme division between the Southern classes has made many a good literary characterization.

To understand the Southerner you must know that there are really two Souths in which he lives. These two Souths, the "Old South" and the "New South," are as different as night and day, yet both are as "Southern as Southern can be."

The "Old South" of pre-Civil War days is no more, but strong remnants survive in the "old families" and in their beliefs. There is something very nostalgic and romantic about the Old South.

The Old South lives in areas where there has not been much industry and where the aftermath of slavery made major changes in the great mansions and plantations. In the Old South the industry remains in raw materials such as tobacco, cotton, rice, corn and peanuts.

The Old South is symbolized by mansions like "Tara," by Stone Mountain with its profiles of Jefferson Davis, Lee and Jackson, and by the double-barreled cannon on the courthouse square in Athens, Georgia. (This dual cannon was to shoot out two balls, each connected by a chain, from its twin barrels. These linked balls were to mow down the enemy, but instead, acted

4

as a boomerang. It was a valiant try.) It is symbolized by the Capitol of the Confederacy on Goat Hill in Montgomery, Alabama; by the classic capitol building in Columbia, South Carolina, still pockmocked by Sherman's cannon; and, of course, by "Old Charleston," in itself the epitome of the Southern way of life, a town opposed to change.

The "New South" is really the "Industrialized South." It produces manufactured goods such as textiles, cigarettes, furniture, radios, televisions, soft drinks, atomic bombs and space technology.

The New South lives in cities, is energetic and on the move.

The New South is symbolized by Birmingham, Alabama, a city built by steel after the Civil War; by the National Aeronautic and Space Administration (NASA) centers in Houston, Texas, and Cape Canaveral, Florida; and by the cattle barons and oilionaires in Texas.

The New South is always building or buying houses, while the Old South was born with one. The New South judges people by the money they make and the part of town in which they live. The Old South doesn't ask a man what he has but must know who his folks are. The New South works hard while the Old South takes it easy. The New South would rather play golf, while the Old South goes fishing.

Is it true what they say about Dixie? Yes. No. Maybe.

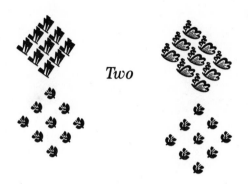

Two

THE SOUTHERNER'S ENGLISH

THE SOUTHERNER DIALECT is not really Southern at all, but the Queen's English of the time of Queen Elizabeth I, Shakespeare, Marlowe, Walter Raleigh, Addison, Swift, Pope, Dryden, Bacon and Boswell. Elizabethan words and expressions are common today throughout the South. Unlike Shakespeare's prose, though, the Southerner's words and phrases are devised for function, not beauty. However, if Shakespeare were to travel into the remote regions of North Carolina today, into the coves and hollows of the Blue Ridge and Great Smoky Mountains, he would find highlanders conversing in his own pure mother tongue (although heavily accented), and he would have no difficulty at all fitting in.

The highlanders are mountain people who came from the British Isles during the eighteenth century. They settled in the Great Smoky Mountains of Tennessee and North Carolina, the Cumberlands of Tennessee and Kentucky, the Blue Ridge Mountains of the Virginias and the Ozark Mountains of Arkansas and Missouri.

The highlanders have changed relatively little in two hundred years. They are a hardy people who build their own homes, make their own clothes, do their own doctoring and rely on nature and their families for their education. They are survivors. However, now that civilization has forced itself on them, the younger generation is adopting the speech and ways of their teachers and co-workers. The older folks, even today, are skeptical and cautious about changes in their way of life and speech and most choose to retain their colorful highland dialect, a speech so filled with intonation that it is almost melodic.

It is here in Possum Holler with the highlanders that Shakespeare would feel at home.

Southerners are proud of their background and of their speech, and even though "General American Middle Western Speech" dominates the airwaves in radio and television and on film as a role model, the Southerner retains his own dialect as a matter of pride.

The average educated "upper class" Southerner speaks with almost the same grammatical correctness as the average Northerner. The "lower class" or less educated Southerner will be more lax in his speech and it will contain an abundance of grammatical errors. Southern speech is not necessarily correct or incorrect, however, but is often filled with colorful words and phrases that, whether grammatically acceptable or not, are widely used by all Southerners.

The following are some of the more common grammar changes to be noted:

1. Three major hallmarks of Southern speech, the substitution of "AH" for "I," "MAH" for "MY" and the dropping of "G's" at the end of words, are not a result of a lazy tongue or a holdover from darkest Africa, but from fashionable London, thanks to the Virgin Queen. These three are spoken dialect traits but are often written this way, especially the dropping of "G's."

2. The double negative is often heard (and was a favorite of Queen Elizabeth's). *IT DON'T MAKE NO NEVERMIND. WE DON'T NONE OF US NEED TO GO.*

3. *"HIT" (another of the Queen's favorites) is often used in place of "IT." HIT'S A COMIN' ON TO RAIN.*

4. *"Y' ALL" is an expression common to the entire South. It is intended to refer to the plural (YOU ALL), but some highlanders use it in the singular. Y' ALL ARE LOOKIN' MIGHTY FINE, DARLIN'.*

5. *Verb forms are often misused. WE HAS ALL WE NEED.*

6. *Adverbs "HERE" and "THERE" are overused. THIS HERE'S THE PLACE. THAT THERE MAN'S MINE.*

7. *"AN" is often replaced by "A." I'LL BE DONE IN A HOUR.*

8. *"FOR" is often used after verbs. I DON'T INTEND FOR HIM TO GO.*
9. *In a sentence with two verbs, the second is often changed into an infinitive by the addition of "TO." I'LL HAVE JANE TO CALL HIM FOR YOU.*
10. *"TO" is often substituted for "AT." I SHOP TO JONES'S MARKET.*
11. *Rural and mountain folk often use "DONE" in place of "HAVE" or "HAS." I DONE TOLD YOU NOT TO DO THAT.*
12. *Highlanders are fond of repeating themselves. Some of the more common compounds are: HOUNDDOG, MAN PERSON, BIBLE BOOK, GRANNY WOMAN, RIFLE GUN, KID OF A BOY, TOOTH DENTIST and BISCUIT BREAD.*
13. *Other examples of this redundancy are: SHE GENERALLY, USUALLY REMEMBERS IT. HE WAS A TEENY TINY LITTLE PUNY OLD THING.*
14. *"AS" often replaces "THAT," "THAN" and "WHO." I DON'T KNOW AS I EVEN CARE. I'D RATHER DANCE AS EAT. HE'S THE ONE AS BROKE IT.*
15. *"A" (UH) is frequently used before verbs ending in "ING." I'M A-GITTIN' TO IT. NO NEED TO GO A-HOLLERIN'.*
16. *Adjectives and nouns are often used as verbs. SHE PRETTIED HERSELF UP SOME. I'LL MUSCLE IT UP FOR YOU.*
17. *"EST" is often added to the present participle.*

HE'S THE WORKINGEST MAN I KNOW.

18. *Compounds are often reversed. TAKE EVERWHICH ONE YOU FANCY.*
19. *"LIKE" is often added to words. HE LOOKS SORRY-LIKE AND LONESOME-LIKE.*
20. *When "LIKE" is used as a verb, it is often followed by "FOR." I'D LIKE FOR YOU TO COME ALONG.*
21. *The verb "LISTEN" is often followed by "AT." I'M GONNA LISTEN AT THE RADIO SOME.*
22. *Personal pronouns are frequently added after the subject noun. SUE, SHE IS A PRETTY ONE.*

In the following chapters you will find words and phrases and their meanings. These are not labeled to show their grammatical correctness.

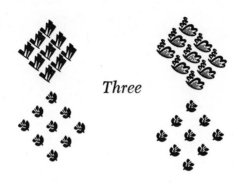

Three

SOUTHERN WORDS

ACTABLE: Lively. *He's a right actable ole man.*

ADDLED: Confused, disoriented. *I can't make hide nor hair out of this map and it's got me right addled.*

AFEERED: Afraid. *The little 'uns are afeered of the dark.*

AFORE: Before. *Better bring the wash in afore it storms up.*

A FIXIN': Preparing. *I'm a fixin' to go.*

AIM: Plan. *I aim to please.*

AIN'T: Is not. *Ain't no way to treat a lady.*

ALL-OVERS: Exhaustion. *I worked so hard I've got the all-overs.*

ALLUS: Always. *I allus wanted me one of them new-fangled carry bags.*

ARTHURITIS: Arthritis. *My arthuritis is actin' up again.*

ARY: Any. *Take ary one you've a mind to.*

ASHY: Angry. *He was too dang ashy to listen to reason.*

A'TALL: At all. *I ain't heered nothin' a'tall.*

AWFULLEST: The worst. *That's the awfullest joke I ever did hear.*

AX: Ask. *They axed us were we goin'.*

BACCER: Tobacco. *He thought on it some as he took out his baccer pouch and filled his pipe.*

BACK: Address a letter. *I've got to back a letter and get it to post.*

BACKJAW: Backtalk. *Don't give your pa no backjaw.*

15

BAD-MOUTH: To speak negatively to or about some-one. *All he does is bad-mouth the boss.*

BALD: Treeless mountain. *He had him a shack t'other side of bald mountain.*

BANJO-BELLY: A man with a pot belly. *Ernie's an ole banjo-belly who loves his beer.*

BARNIN': Harvesting. *I 'spect he'll show up lookin' for work 'round barnin' time.*

BEE GUM: Beehive. *He heard the bee gum afore he saw it.*

BELLYWASHER: Beverage. *I need me a bellywasher after eatin' all them catfish.*

BEST: Better. *You best get that mess cleaned up.*

BIB 'N' TUCKER: Overalls. *Put on your best bib 'n' tucker and let's go to town.*

BIDDIE: Baby chick. *The old hen and her biddies marched 'round the yard.*

BIGGETY: Snobbish. *She ain't nothin' but a biggety ole spinster.*

BLACK ANNIE: Police wagon. *After the brawl every-one was hauled away in the Black Annie.*

BLESS OUT: Cuss out. *When he comes home Pa's gonna bless out Sam but good.*

BLINKY: Sour. *I have to return the blinky milk to the store.*

BOLL WEEVIL: Insect that feeds on the cotton plant. *That ole boll weevil'll put a man under sure as nothin'.*

BONE CARRIER: A gossip. *She's an ole bone carrier an' she's got no business 'round here.*

BOOK-LARNIN': Education. *I ain't had no book-larnin' but I knows me a mite more than those ole desk farmers.*

BOUGHTEN: Purchased. Not home-made. *He gave her a boughten dress for her birthday.*

BOWDACIOUS: Smart-aleck. Show off. *I got me a right bowdacious coon dog.*

BOY: Southern, white, beer drinking, fun-loving male. *Those good ole boys are gonna have some fun tonight.*

BRANCH: Small stream of water. *He followed the branch 'till he reached the creek.*

BRAR: Briar. *We soon learned to steer clear of the*

brar patch.

BRARPATCH CHILD: Illegitimate. *She slept on the wrong side of the blanket and now she has a brar-patch child to raise.*

BREAKDOWN: Square dance. *We're goin' to a breakdown tonight.*

BRITCHES: Pants. *He tore his britches when he backed into the brarpatch.*

BROGANS: Shoes. *Come winter we all got a new pair of brogans.*

BUCK DANCIN': A cross between an Irish jig and tap dancing. *Pa got out his fiddle and set Ma to buck dancin'.*

BUCK 'N' WING: Another term for buck dancing.

BUCK OUT: Figure out. *We tried to buck out the map directions.*

BUNK: Talk for talk's sake. *That's a lot of bunk. You can't fix that rig anymore than I can.*

BURIN: A funeral. *There was a bruin for ole Ezra on up to the church.*

BUSS: Kiss. *He bussed her quickly and ran off to join his friends.*

BUT: Only. *Ain't but one left.*

BUTT: An abrupt end of a mountain. *He stood at the butt and looked out over the valley.*

CAKE WALK: Musical game. Partners walk around the room until the music stops. The couple nearest a pre-chosen spot wins a cake. *There was a cake walk and a pie judgin' goin' on at the social.*

CALL: Reason. *You ain't got no call to act like that.*

CARRY: Take. *Carry me home.*

CARRY BAG: Tote bag, shopping bag. *She came home with her carry bag full of pralines.*

CATCHALL: A drawer filled with lots of odds and ends. *If'n you can't find somethin', look in the catchall.*

CAT HEADS: Biscuits. *Granny cooked up cat heads and gravy for supper.*

CATTYMOUNT: A fearful creature. *She heard a cattymount in the night.*

CAUTION: Something else, a real joker. *Ain't he a caution?*

CHAW: Chewing tobacco. *He allus has a chaw in his*

jaw

CHIGGERS: Mites whose larvae stick to the skin and cause severe itching. *You chillen stay out of the woods or the chiggers 'll get you.*

CHILLEN (also CHIREN):   Children. *Them chillen's up to no good.*

CHIMLEY: Chimney. *Birds is allus nestin' in the chimley.*

CHUNK: Throw. *I've got to chunk all these papers out.*

CITIFIED: Urbanized. *He's lookin' right citified in his new britches.*

CLAPHAT: Hasty. *She was a claphat woman, allus sayin' things she hadn't ought to.*

CLATTERBOX: Someone who talks too much. *Miz Addie, she's a right clatterbox, she is.*

CLIM: Climbed. *He clim up the ladder.*

CLODHOPPER: Clumsy farm boy. *He was a country bumpkin, a clodhopper.*

CLOG: A dance performed with clogs (wooden shoes), characterized by heavy stamping steps. *The cloggers traveled all over the country with their show.*

CLONE: Cologne. *That's mighty nice clone you're wearing, Miz Suzanna.*

CLUM: Past tense of climb. *He clumb up on the roof.*

COAL OIL: Kerosene. *The coal oil was in short supply that winter.*

COAL YARD: Black coffee. *Pour the coal yard and make it quick.*

CO-COLA: Coca-cola. *Grandma sure did love her co-colas.*

COMB: Ridgepole on a roof. *He put a weather vane on the comb of the house.*

COMEUPPANCE: Just rewards. *He played one trick too many and got his comeuppance.*

COMFORT: Quilted blanket. *She pulled up the kivers and comfort.*

COMMODE: Toilet. *The little 'uns were real taken with the new commode and kept pullin' on the chain.*

COMPANY: Guests. *Company's comin'.*

CONJOINING: Connecting. *They had conjoining*

rooms in the hotel.

CONJURE: Build or make up. *Don't conjure up any more trouble.*

COON: Racoon. *We're goin' coon huntin'.*

COON ASS: Derogatory slang for Cajun. *Them swamps is full of coon asses.*

COON DOG: Racoon hunting dog. *I've got the best coon dogs in the county.*

COOTER: Large fresh water turtle. *There's some says cooters make fine soup.*

COTTON: Like or agree. *I don't cotton to that.*

COUNTRY BUMPKIN: Naive rural resident. *Don't be such a country bumpkin.*

COURSE: Follow. *He coursed the hounddog straight to the rabbit.*

COVE: A widening out of a mountain or valley. *They camped in the cove.*

COVERALLS: Overalls. Bibbed jeans. *He pulled on his boots and coveralls and headed for the fields.*

CRACKER: Southern, white, poor folks, rednecks. So poor they have only crackers and cheese for meals.

Most often the term used is "Georgia cracker." *Those Georgia crackers don't take well to long-haired hippies.*

CREEK: Larger than a branch. *They went wadin' in the creek.*

CRITTER: Small animal. *Those kittens are cute little critters.*

CROUP: A cough. *He took down with the croup and had to be tended to.*

DAGNABBIT: Exclamation. *Dagnabbit, boy, get that thing out of here!*

DANDER: Dandruff. Excited. *Don't get your dander up.*

DANG: Exclamation. *Dang! Don't that beat all!*

DAYDAWN: Daybreak. *He was up before daydawn and down to the fishin' hole.*

DEAH: Dear. *Oh, deah me!*

DEVILMENT: Playful trouble. *Those kids are into more devilment again.*

DEVIL'S RIDING HORSE: Praying mantis. *I'm afeered of devil's riding horses and dragonflies.*

DINNER: They midday meal. *She was settin' out the vittles for dinner.*

DISREMEMBER: Don't remember. *I disremember what all happened.*

DIRECTLY: Soon. *I'll get to it directly.*

DITCH-EDGE CHILD: Illegitimate child. *They had them another ditch-edge child to feed.*

DITTY-BOP HAT: A beret with a brim. *He pulled his ditty-bop hat low to cover the haircut his mama had given him.*

DOFUNNIES: Knick-knacks. *She had a lot of them dofunnies on a shelf.*

DOHICKIES: Also knick-knacks or any small article. *The hat had some sparkly dohickies on it.*

DONNYBROOK: A fight. *They got into a real donnybrook with everyone in the bar joining in.*

DOWNRIGHT: Very. *He was downright rude.*

DRINKIN' LIQUOR: Smooth whiskey. *No shine tonight, we've got some real fine drinkin' liquor.*

DRUTHER: I'd rather. *Druther you go now.*

DRUTHERS: Choice. *If I had my druthers, I'd buy*

me one of them blue caps.

DRY COUNTY: A throwback to Prohibition. Many Souther counties remain "dry" today. No liquor can be purchased by the drink or by the bottle.

DRY GRIN: Embarrassed grin. *There he was with a dry grin and a jug 'o shine.*

DUDS: Clothes. *Them's nice duds you're wearin'.*

DUMB SUPPER: Old wives' tale. Young folks who wish to find their future mates eat a meal, in silence, of cornbread made with equal parts of meal and salt. No one speaks the rest of the evening. The dreams that follow this salty repast will disclose the dreamer's future spouse, who will appear with a drink of water.

DURN: Exclamation. *Durn! I should have gone too.*

DUSTY-DARK: Time before twilight sky turns from gray to blue. *Best get home afore dusty-dark or you'll miss your supper.*

EGG-ON: Provoke. *If'n you egg him on he'll turn on you.*

EVENING: Time after 12:00 noon—rather than "afternoon."

EVER: Every. *Ever one of them showed up for*

supper.

EVERHOO: Reverse of whoever. *Everhoo one of you wants, come on.*

FAR: Fire. *The far was blazing.*

FAR BOARD: Fireplace mantel. *The baccer tote is on the bar board.*

FAULT: Blame. *Can't fault him for that.*

FAVOR: Resemble. *He favors his father.*

FEISTY: Conceited. Showoff. *He had a feisty little dog.*

FELLER: Fellow. Boy. *He's a right mannered feller.*

FELL OFF: Lost weight. *She fell off some and is lookin' right good.*

FER PIECE: A long way away. *They live a fer piece down the road.*

FETCH: Bring. *Fetch me the jug.*

FETCHIN':   Attractive. *She's real fetchin'.*

FIT: Fought. *They fit till they were plumb wore out.*

FITTIN':   In condition, entitled. *He ain't fitten to be seen.*

FLOG: An attack of an angry hen or person. *The hen flogged the intruding weasel.*

FLYIN' JENNY: Merry-go-round. *The young'uns are over to the flyin' jenny.*

FOLKS   People. *Folks are none too friendly 'round these parts.*

FOOL: Darn. *Ever fool thing went wrong.*

FOORAW: A party or gathering. *That was some swell fooraw last night.*

FOXFIRE: A fungus in decayed wood that causes a phosphorescent glow. *They watched the foxfire and fire flies by the creek.*

FRAY: Brawl. *He was allus in the middle of the fray.*

FRESH: New. *I bought it fresh.*

FRET: Fuss. Worry. *It's nothing to fret on.*

FURRINER: Foreigner or stranger. *Most people don't confidence furriners.*

GAILY: Spirited. Healthy. *She's acting awful gaily today.*

GAL: Girl. *Bless the gal's heart.*

GALLERY: Porch. *She's sittin' on the gallery shuckin' goobers.*

GAYSOME: Happy. Frolicsome. *They are mighty gaysome puppies.*

GENTEEL: Upper class, wealthy. *They're acting mighty genteel.*

GENTEEL POVERTY: With possessions, but financially poor. *She lived in genteel poverty in the heavily mortgaged house she inherited from her parents.*

GIGGLE-SOUP: Alcholic beverage, usually homemade moonshine or wine. *They drank so much giggle-soup they couldn't hardly stand up.*

GO-DOWN: Sickly. Not well. *She's been on the go-down for some time.*

GOLDRUN: Darn. *The goldurn battery's dead.*

GOOD-COUNTENANCED: Good-natured. *She a good-countenanced teacher.*

GRANNY: A grandmother. *Granny tended the young'uns while Ma cooked.*

GRANNY-WOMAN: A midwife. *The granny-woman*

has come to help with the birthin'.

GRASS: Spring. *We'll plant in grass time.*

GRAVEYARD CLEANING: Annual affair at country churches. After a picnic (dinner on the ground) the church members clean the cemetery, digging up weeds, propping up sagging tombstones, and decorating with flowers.

GREEN: Tease. *Don't green her.*

GROSS: Complain. *He was grossin' 'bout goin' to school.*

GUMPTION: Initiative. Guts. *He's got the gumption for the job.*

GUY SCOOTER-SKY: A steer with hind legs longer than fore legs for mountain grazing.

HAINT: Ghost. *The haints are out tonight.*

HANDILY: Honestly. *I don't handily know the reason for it.*

HANKER: Want. *I hanker to have me one.*

HARDNESS: Ill-feeling. *I don't harbor no hardness against you.*

HARP: Harmonica or mouth harp. *We got out the*

harp and the fiddle and had us a hoe-down.

HAYMAKER: A knock-out punch. *They were in a knock-down-drag-out when he laid on his haymaker.*

HEAP: A great deal. *It takes a heap o' work to plow that field.*

HEIST: To raise. *Heist the ladder to the loft.*

HEP: Help. *Can I hep you to some coffee and cake?*

HERN: Hers. *The puppy was hern from the moment she laid eyes on it.*

HEY: Hello. *Hey, Andy, how are you?*

HICK: Slang for backwards, rural, unsophisticated person or town. *He came from a hick town that wasn't even on the bus line.*

HILLBILLY: Slang for a person from the backwoods or remote mountain areas. *The old hillbilly had no use for any newfangled gadgets.*

HILLWILLIAM: A hillbilly who's "gone to town," "earned enough to hire a lawyer," "wears running shoes and golf shirts," etc.

HIPPINS: Diapers. *Pin the hippins on that young'un afore he crawls away in the altogether.*

HISN: His. *This one's hisn and that one's yourn.*

HISSY FIT: Tantrum. *She's stompin' 'round in a real hissy fit.*

HIT: It. *Hit don't make no nevermind.*

HITCHED: Married. *The preacher hitched 'em.*

HOARFROST: A delicate white coating of ice crystals covering the trees and ground like dew that melts quickly at the first suggestion of warm sun. *The hoarfrost crunched as he walked through the field.*

HOE-DOWN: Party. *The neighbors all came to the hoe-down*

HOLLER: Yell. Scream. *Don't holler so.* Also, hollow. *They lived in the holler.*

HONEY CHILE: Honey Child. *Honey chile, don't you fret none.*

HONKY-TONK: Southern bar, with country band, pool tables and lots of fun. *The most famous honky-tonks are Gilley's in Houston, Texas, Billy Bob's in Dallas-Ft. Worth, Texas, and the Palomino in North Hollywood, California.*

HONKY-TONKIN': Going out for an evening at the local honky-tonk. *We're goin' honky-tonkin' tonight.*

HOPE: Past tense of help. *I hope him with his chores.*

HOW COME: Why. *How come you didn't call?*

HOWEVER: No matter how. *However you do it, she doesn't like it.*

HUMUNGOUS: Very big. *Buddy ran through the field and came face to face with a humungous bull.*

HUNKER: Squat. *Hunker down and fetch me that bucket.*

ICE PEBBLES: Hail. *Ice pebbles were bouncing off the car.*

ILL: Angry. *He's ill as a hornet.*

IT: Baby. Rather than refer to a baby by its gender, it is commonplace to call the baby "it." *Does it want its bottle?*

JACKLEG: Self-educated. Usually refers to automobile mechanics and clergymen. *My truck was workin' fine till that ole jackleg mechanic got a hold of it.*

JACKRABBITER: A moonshiner who uses inferior equipment instead of pure copper pans and tubing (sometimes even running the shine through car radiators) and adding chemicals to speed up the fermenting of the mash. The moonshine a jackrabbiter produces can very often be poinsonous. A jackrabbiter will run into an area, make his shine, sell it and leave before there is any trouble. Most people will not buy from anyone but a moonshiner who is well known and trusted.

JANDERS: Jaundice. *He was yeller with janders.*

JAWDY: Talkative. *Hector's too jawdy for his own good.*

JOHNBOAT: Flat bottom boat. Holds two to four people and is propelled by one person standing up in the boat using a long pole to touch the river bottom.

JOOK JOINT: Honky-tonk bar with a juke box. *He runs an ole jook joint out on I-5.*

JOURNEY PROUD: Enthusiasm resulting from a trip. *She was so journey proud when she returned from her trip that she couldn't stop talking about it.*

JULARKER: Boyfriend. *The young lady's jularker came callin'.*

KIN: And kinfolk. An Elizabethan expression meaning relatives. *She has a lot of kinfolk.*

KIVER: Bed cover. Blanket. *He slipped under the kiver and went to sleep.*

KNEE-WALKING: Drunk. *He got real knee-walking after he got fired.*

KNOB: Mountaintop. *The boys planned a hike to the knob.*

KNUCKLEBUSTER: Fist fight. *The boys were into a real knucklebuster by the time the police arrived.*

LADY'S SLIPPERS: A warm climate orchid. *She gathered lady's slippers and mountain laurel for decoration.*

LATCH: To close or put a lid on. Also, to grab on to. *Latch the screen door when you leave.*

LATCH PIN: Safety pin. *Hand me some latch pins for the baby's hippins.*

LAW: Sue. *I'll law him in court.*

LEARN: Teach. *I'll learn him a thing or two.*

LEVEE: A pier or river embankment. *Let's go fishin' down by the levee.*

LIGHTWOOD: Kindling. *We need more lightwood for the far.*

LIGHTING WOOD: Same as above.

LIGHTER KNOTS: Same as above.

LIKE TO: Almost. *I like to broke my back.*

LIL: Small, little. *What a cute lil thing!*

LINT-DODGER: Mill worker. *I could never be a lint-dodger at the mercy of a time clock and a strawboss.*

LITTLE'UNS: Children. *The little'uns are asleep.*

LORDY: Exclamation. Good Lord. *Lordy, Miz Brown, you can really cook.*

LOW: Sound made by contented cows. *The cattle are lowing.*

LOWGROUND: Low lying land, usually near a body of water. *He bought some fine lowground.*

MA'AM: Madam. *Thank you kindly, ma'am.*

MATERS: Tomatoes. *Pass the maters 'n' taters.*

MENFOLK: Men. *The menfolk will be home afore long.*

MERCY: Exclamation. *Mercy! Is that present for me?*

MESS: A lot. *She cooked a mess of grits.*

MIDDLIN': Midway. So-so. *Feelin' middlin'.* Also, a side of bacon. *She cooked up a mess of eggs and middlin.*

MIGHT COULD: Might be able to. *I might could help you.*

MIGHTY: Very. *That's mighty nice of you.*

MIGHTY NIGH: Very nearly. *It's mighty nigh burnt out.*

MIND: Remember. *Mind your manners.* Also, attention. *If she cries pay her no mind.*

MIRIN' BRANCH: Quicksand stream. *The dog was caught in a mirin' branch.*

MISSY: Miss. *Don't backjaw me, missy.*

MITE: A bit. *Wait a mite.*

MIZ: Mrs. *Miz Callie's piccalilli won first prize at the fair.*

MOONSHINE: Illegally distilled liquor.

MOONSHINER: A person who operates an illegal still. Moonshining is a serious business and those who distill good "shine" can make a good living at it, if they aren't caught by the revenuers.

MORNGLOAM: First light of day. *When morngloam broke, he was already in the field.*

MOSQUITO HAWK: Dragonfly. *The mosquito hawks scared him.*

MOTHER HUBBARD: Long apron with bib. *She put on her mother hubbard and set to cookin'.*

MOTHER WIT: Natural intelligence, common sense. *Beulah was not an educated woman but she had mother wit.*

MOUGHT: Might. *I mought go fishin'.*

MOUNTAIN LAUREL: Evergreen shrub with rose or white flowers. *Mountain laurel grows wild higher up the mountain.*

MUCH: Praise. *Why don't you much me instead of faulting me?*

MULLYGRUBS: Sulks. *She had the mullygrubs on it.*

MURDERSOME HOT: Very hot. *It's so murdersome hot not even the mosquitos are out.*

MUSCLE UP: Lift up. *Muscle up that bale of hay yonder.*

NARY: Not any. *He owns nary a thing but the clothes on his back.*

NEUMONIE FEVER: Pneumonia. *He took down with neumonie fever.*

NEWFANGLED: New item. *Give me one of them newfangled baccer pokes.*

NEW GROUND: Newly cleared farm land. *He set to tillin' the new ground.*

NIGH ON: Almost. *It's nigh on to midnight.*

NONE: At all. *It won't hurt you none.*

NOACCOUNT: Lazy. Shiftless. A bum. *He's a noaccount drifter.*

NO NEVERMIND: Difference. *It don't make no nevermind.*

NUBBIN: Small ear of corn that grows on the top of the cornstalk. *The nubbins were saved for cattlefeed.*

NUSS: Hold. *Nuss the baby.*

OFFISH: Reserved. *She's a mite offish.*

OFF'N: From. *I took it off'n him.*

OLE: Old. *The ole boy's gonna have some fun tonight.*

ONE: (Or the other). *You're gonna clean your room or get whupped one.*

ORATE: Speak. *Hush your mouth when I is oratin'.*

ORNAMENTS: Jewelry. *She was dressed fit to kill with all her ornaments.*

ORNERY: Disagreeable, gruff. *He's an ornery ole man.*

OUTHOUSE: Also backhouse or shanty. A toilet housed in a small, wooden shed. *In winter the outhouse seemed miles away.*

OUTLANDER: Stranger. Foreigner. *He eyed the outlander comin' up the holler.*

OUT'N: Out of. *I took it out'n the box.*

OVERHALLS: Overalls. Bibbed jeans. *Jake's got but one pair of overhalls.*

OWNLIEST: The only one. *He's the ownliest one for me.*

PACKAGE STORE: Small grocery store. *Run on down to the package store for me.*

PALLET: Make-shift bed. *Ma made pallets on the floor for the company.*

PARTS: Area. *We don't cotton to strangers in these parts.*

PASSEL: A lot of something. *They've got a passel o'l young'uns.*

PATCH: Field or garden. *Pa's tillin' in the patch.*

PEEK-BY-NIGHT: Flower that opens at night. *She stayed up to see the peek-by-nights.*

PERT: Very active. *Your granny's a right pert lady.*

PICAYUNISH: Nit picking. Particular. *You're being very picayunish about this.*

PIDDLE DIDDLE: To procrastinate. *Don't piddle diddle around when there's chores to be done.*

PIDDLIN': Fooling around. *He's piddlin' in the work shed.* Also small, unimportant. *I have just a piddlin' bit of work left to do.*

PIGGIN': Wooden bucket. *She filled the piggin' with seed.*

PINCH: Snuff. *Don't need no chaw, I've got some pinch.*

PINCHBACK SUIT: Many an unscrupulous salesman has been known to "pinch back"the suit his customer is trying on, so that when the customer looks into the mirror the suit looks like it fits him to a "T." *Elmer thought he was a dandy in his blue plaid pinchback suit.*

PINT: Point. *Ain't got but one more pint to make.*

PITY-SAKE: Pity. *He took pity-sake on her.*

PLUMB: Indicates degree. *I'm plumb wore out.*

POKE: Paper bag or sack. *She had a poke full of raspberries.* Also green vegetable, like spinach. *Poke grows wild in these parts.*

POKE SALLET: Poke salad. *Poke sallet was all they had for supper.*

POKIN': Leisurely walk. *She's pokin' along to school.*

POLECAT: Skunk. *We tried to play with the polecat and learned not to.*

POOR: Skinny. Slender. *He's so poor his coveralls are hangin' on him.*

POSSUM: Opossum. *We're havin' a possum hunt tonight.*

POWER: A greal deal. *He had a power of money.*

POWERFUL: Very. Tremendously. *That was powerful good.*

PREACHER: Minister of the gospel. *Preacher Jones was well liked.*

PRIZE: Pull. *We had to prize the boys apart to stop the fight.*

PUFFED UP: Mad. *Don't get puffed up about it.*

PULLEY-BONE: Wish bone. Old custom has it that if a young girl places the short end of the pulley-bone above the doorway, the first boy that walks through the door will be the one she marries.

PUNY: Small, undeveloped. *He's the puny runt of the litter.* Also, not well. *I'm feelin sort of puny lately.*

PURSH: Push. *Pursh harder!*

PURTY GOOD: Just fine. *I'm doin' purty good.*

QUARE: Queer. Strange. *He's a quare old man.*

QUART JUICE: Moonshine or homemade fruit liquor. *Pappy was known for his blackberry quart juice.*

QUICK SACK: Corner liquor/grocery store. *He ran to the quick sack for beer.*

QUIETUS: Calm period in early morning or late afternoon when chores are done. *She longed for the quietus.*

QUILTIN' BEE: A quilt sewing party where many

women get together and sew, each taking a section, until the quilt is finished. *Ma loved the quiltin' bees because she got a chance to hear all the latest gossip.*

RAINSEED: Brownish, mottled clouds. *The rainseed are forming.*

RARE BACK: Lean back and prepare to make a move. *He rared back and let out a yell to surprise the intruder.*

RIGHT: Very. *That was right nice.*

RECEIPT: Recipe. *I want the receipt for that pie of yourn.*

RECKON: Guess. *Reckon you know what you're doing.*

REDBUGS: Chiggers. *Stay out of the bushes or the redbugs'll get you.*

REDDIN' UP: Cleaning up. *I've got some reddin' up to do afore we go.*

REDNECK: The term came from the farmers, the plowboys, who plow in the hot sun with their heads down, exposing the backs of their necks to the sun. *Ole Jim's a true redneck who spends all day followin' the south end of a northbound mule.* The term now generally refers to the good ole boys who love their drinkin', women, huntin', fishin', God and country, and are quick to vocally and physically defend all of the above.

RETCH: Reach. *I can't retch it.*

REVENOOR: Revenuer. Federal agent who must locate and dismantle illegal moonshine stills and arrest the moonshiners.

RID: Rode. *He rid into town.*

RIMPTIONS: Plenty. *We have rimptions of them.*

RUINATION: Ruin. *He'll be the ruination of me.*

SALLET: Fresh vegetables, lettuce. *There's plenty of greens for sallet.*

SASS: Elizabethan term meaning saucy, impertinent. *Don't sass me, young lady.* Also means weeds. *She's gettin' sass out of the garden.*

SAWDUST HEAD: Not an intelligent person. *He was a real sawdust head about farming.*

SCROOCH: Move over and make room. *Scrooch a bit so's I can fit in.*

SCUPPERNONG: Muscadine variety grape. *The Ames sisters only make scuppernong wine.*

SEE FIT: Care to. *You're welcome to join us if you*

see fit.

SET IN: Begin. *Darkness set in before he could make it home.*

SHACKLIN': Feel under the weather. *I've been feelin' sort o' shacklin' lately.*

SHADDER: Shadow. *He was skeered of his own shadder.*

SHEEIT!: Exclamation. Shit!

SHINDIG: Party. *That was some shindig last night.*

SHINE: Moonshine liquor. *Zeb makes the best shine in the county.*

SHITKICKER: Rural resident or troublemaker. *That tavern is full of shitkickers and clodhoppers.*

SHIVAREE: A mock serenade with kettles, pans, horns and other noise-makers given for a newly married couple.

SHOE BREAD: A thin sandwich of bread and bacon. *The young'uns went off to school barefoot and with a shoe bread each.*

SHOOT: For belittlement. *Shoot, that ain't nothin'.*

SHORE: Sure. *I ain't shore 'o nothin'.*

SHORT-SWEETENING: Sugar. *She used lots of short-sweetening in her cakes.*

SHOT-GUN HOUSE: House built on one level with rooms all in a row. *They lived in a shot-gun house at the end of the holler.*

SHUCK: To remove husk. *She's been shucking corn.*

SIDLE UP: Get close to. *He sidled up to Amy but she didn't pay him no mind.*

SKEERED: Scared. Frightened. *I ain't skeered o' none o' his kind.*

SLAM: Completely. *He slam bought out the store.*

SLAP: Plainly, simply. *He slap quit his job.*

SLIPPERSLIDE: Shoe horn. *I need a slipperslide to get these boots on.*

SLOP BUCKET: Bucket kept in the kitchen into which leftovers of the day's meals are stored and later fed to the hogs. *She cleared the table and filled the slop bucket.*

SLUE: A large amount. *He had a slue of hens for sale.*

SMIDGEN: A small amount. *There's just a smidgen*

of pie left.

SMUDGE: A very small amount. *She had only a smudge of cream.*

SMOLLYGOSTER: A political candidate who wants office regardless of party, platform or principles. *That old smollygoster is talkin' bunk.*

SNAKE DOCTOR: Dragonfly. Also called mosquito hawks. *The snake doctors were flying everywhere.*

SNEAKY PETE: Moonshine. *He took a swig of Sneaky Pete before heading home.*

SNORT: Swig, drink. *He takes a snort now and then.*

SNUFF: Finely pulverized tobacco drawn into the nostrils by inhaling. *He took a pinch of snuff now and then.*

SNUFF CHEWER: Rural resident. *How is the old snuff chewer?*

SOCIAL: A party and dance held on the grounds of the church or school. *All the neighbors and kinfolk came to the social.*

SORRY: Lazy. *He's one sorry boy.*

SOT: Alcoholic. *He was a noaccount sot.*

SPARKIN': Dating. *Granny told us stories about her sparkin' days.*

SPELL: Strange behavior. *A spell came over her.* Also, a short length of time. *Let's sit a spell.*

SPIDER: Skillet. *She had only one pot and spider to cook dinner with.*

S'POSEN: What if. *S'posen you was to come to the social tonight.*

SPUDDIN': Ambling along. *By then the hikers were spuddin' and pokin'.*

SQUIRRELLY: Unpredictable, eccentric. *He's so squirrelly you never know what he's going to do.*

STEWED: Drunk. *The old sot got stewed.*

STOMPDOWN: Square dance. *There's goin' to be a stompdown tonight.*

STORY: An untruth. *He's tellin' you a story, Pa.*

STRADDLEBUG: Politician. *Election time's the only time that old straddlebug comes 'round.*

STRAWBOSS: Foreman. *The strawboss drove his men hard.*

STUDY: Think. *I've got to study on it.*

STRUT: "Chitlin strut" or "okra strut." A fundraising social at which the greatest percentage of food served is chitlins or okra. The "strut" is a term for the "let it all hang out" type of clogging dance.

SUMMERSET: Summersault. *He did a summerset off the diving board.*

SUMPIN': Something. *Ain't that sumpin'!*

SUN-BALL: Sun. *The sun-ball was high.*

SUPPER: The evening meal. *Wash up for supper, young'uns.*

SUPPLY MAN: General store keeper. *He went down to the quick sack to talk with the supply man.*

SURROUND: Go around. *Surround that puddle in the road.*

SUSPICION: Guess. *I suspicioned it.*

SWEETNIN': Sugar or honey. *I need some sweetnin' for my coffee.*

SWEETFEED: Sweet bran feed for cattle. *He pitched hay and set out sweetfeed.*

SWIG: A small drink of liquor. *I'll take a swig of that.*

49

SWIVET: Hurry. Rush. *He was in a swivet.*

TAR: Tire. *Them tar's mighty low.*

TATERS: Potatoes. *She was diggin' up taters.*

TEENSEY-TINESEY: Very small amount. *She wanted a teensey-tinesey taste of wine.*

THAT THERE: That. *That there girl is mine.*

THIS HERE: This. *This here girl is mine.*

TILL: Turn the soil to prepare for planting. *Pa is tilling the greens patch.*

TISIC: Asthma. *She has the tisic somethin' awful.*

TITLEMENT: Ownership. *They were workin' to get titlement of the land.*

TOLABLE: Fairly well. *I'm feelin' tolable.*

TOP: Mountaintop. *We spotted bear on the top.*

TO-RECKLY: Immediately. *I'll go to-reckly.*

TOTE: To take out or to carry. *I'll tote that for you.*

TOTE SACK: Grocery bag. *The clerk carried her tote sack to her car.*

TOOTH DENTIST: Dentist. *Granny's goin' to the tooth dentist in the mornin'.*

TOW SACK: Burlap bag. *We have a tow sack full of potatoes.*

T'OTHER: The other. *It was either this one or t'other one.*

TROLL: State trooper. *He got pulled over by a troll last night.*

TRUCK: Associate. *We don't truck with no white trash.*

TUCKERED OUT: Tired. *He's plumb tuckered out.*

TWAN'T: It wasn't. *Twan't no use askin'.*

TWIXT: Between. *This is just twixt the two of us.*

VARMIT: Wild animal. *That varmit's in the hen house again.*

VISIT: Talk. *I need to visit with you.*

VITTLES: Food. *Mighty fine vittles, ma'am.*

WAITER: Best man. *He was waiter at his brother's wedding.*

51

WAKE: Settin' up with the corpse. *The family held a wake for old Tom.*

WARE: Wire. *The wind tore the phone wares down.*

WARSH: Wash. *Warsh your hands first.*

WE'UNS: All of us. *It's time we'uns were heading home.*

WHATZAT: What's that? Used as a question or an exclamation. *Whatzat! What the heck is going on here?*

WHICKER: A sound horses make. *The horses whickered and snorted.*

WHIPAROUND: A person who constantly changes his/her mind. *She's such a whiparound we'll never get this party planned.*

WHISTLE-BRITCHES: Small boy proud of his first pair of trousers. *Here comes little whistle-britches.*

WHITELEATHER: Tough. *A whiteleather customer.*

WHITE MULE: Moonshine. *Jeb loaded the wagon with his latest batch of white mule and set out on his rounds.*

WHITEWASH: Thin, white paint. A cover-up. *He tried to whitewash his mistake.*

WHITE TRASH: Riff raff. Worthless, lazy, shiftless person. *They ain't nothin' but poor white trash livin' in yonder shanty.*

WHUPPED: Whipped. *Pa whupped Clyde but good.*

WIDOW WOMAN: Widow. *The old widow woman sat on her porch reading.*

WINDER: Window. *The winder's broke.*

WITCH-WATER: Heat waves on the road. *He drove on toward the witch-water.*

WITCHES: Hickory or switch for whipping. *Pa kept some witches handy.*

WOMENFOLK: Women. *The womenfolk were at a quiltin' bee.*

WON'T: Contraction for "is not," "were not," "will not," etc. *It won't but a bitty coon makin' all that noise.*

WOOD'S COLT: Illegitimate child. *Don't make no difference whether you call him a ditch-edge child or a brarpatch child or a wood's colt, all's the same.*

WORRIED: Tired. *He's all worried out.*

WRITERMAROUSTER: Court order of ejectment.

She got writermarouster on him to force him to leave.

YAHOO: Rural resident. *Them yahoos and snuff chewers are causin' trouble.*

YANKEE: Northerner. Also anyone who is not a Southerner.

YE: You. *I year ye.*

YERE: Your. *Is this yere dog?*

YONDER: In the distance. *He lives yonder.*

YOUNG'UN: Small child. *The young'uns are all fired up and rarin' to go.*

YOURN: Yours. *This one's yourn.*

YOU'UNS: You all. *When do you'uns reckon you'll be back?*

Y'ALL: You all. *Y'all come back now, hear?*

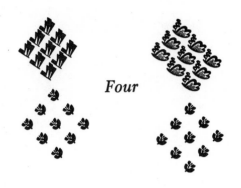

Four

WORDS BY CATEGORY

FOLKS

Boy
Chiren
Chillen
Feller
Folks
Gal
Granny
Hern
Hisn
Little'uns
Ma'am

Menfolk
Missy
Miz
We'uns
Womenfolk
Yankee
Ye
Yere
Young'un
Yourn
You'uns
Y'all

WHAT'S HE/SHE LIKE?

Actable
Biggety
Bone Carrier
Bowdacious
Citified
Clatterbox
Feisty
Gaily
Jackleg
Jawdy
Noaccount
Offish
Picayunish
Quare
Sorry
Squirrelly
Whiparound
Whiteleather

OCCUPATION OR SOCIAL POSITION

Brarpatch Child
Clodhopper
Company
Country Bumpkin
Cracker
Ditch-edge Child
Furriner
Genteel
Granny-woman
Hick
Hillbilly
Hillwilliam
Jackrabbiter
Jularker
Kin
Lint-dodger
Moonshiner
Outlander
Preacher
Redneck
Revenuer
Shitkicker
Smollygoster
Snuff Chewer
Sot
Straddlebug
Strawboss
Supply Man
Tooth Dentist

Words by Category

Troll
Waiter
Whistle-britches
White Trash
Widow Woman
Yahoo

STATE OF MIND

Afeered
Ashy
Gaysome
Good-countenanced
Hissy Fit
Journey Proud
Mullygrubs
Puffed up
Skeered
Swivet

HEALTH

All-overs
Croup
Go-down
Janders
Middlin'
Neumonie Fever
Pert
Purty Good
Shacklin'
Tolable
Tuckered Out
Worried

PHYSICAL APPEARANCE

- Banjo-belly
- Fetchin'
- Humungous
- Poor
- Puny

APPAREL

Bib 'n' Tucker
Britches
Brogans
Coveralls
Ditty-bop Hat
Duds
Mother Hubbard
Overhalls
Pinchback Suit

PARTY TIME

Breakdown
Buck Dancin'
Cake Walk
Clog
Fooraw
Graveyard Cleaning
Hoe-down
Shindig
Shivaree
Social
Stompdown
Strut

LIQUOR

Applejack
Drinkin' Liquor
Giggle-soup
Mint Julep
Moonshine
Quart Juice
Sneaky Pete
Scuppernong Wine
White Mule

TOBACCO

Baccer
Chaw
Pinch
Snuff

EXCLAMATIONS

Dagnabbit!
Dang!
Deah!
Durn!
Goldurn!
Lordy!
Mercy!
Sheeit!
Shoot!
Whatzat!

PLACES

Bald Mountain
Branch
Brar
Butt
Comb
Cove
Creek
Gallery
Honky-Tonk
Jook Joint
Knob
Levee
Low Ground
New Ground
Patch
Top
Yonder

THINGS

Bee Gum
Bellywasher
Black Annie
Carry Bag
Catchall
Cat Heads
Chimley
Clone
Coal Oil
Co-cola
Comfort
Dander
Dofunnies
Dohickies
Far Board
Flyin' Jenny
Gallery
Haint
Harp
Hippins
Ice Pebbles
It
Johnboat
Kiver
Lady's Slippers
Latch Pin
Lightwood
Lightning Wood
Lighter Knots

Maters
Mountain Laurel
Nubbin
Ornaments
Outhouse
Pallet
Peek-by-night
Piggin'
Poke
Poke Sallet
Pulley-bone
Quiltin' Bee
Rainseed
Receipt
Roshn Ears
Sallet
Sass
Scuppernong
Shadder
Shoe Bread
Short-sweetening
Shot-gun House
Slipperslide
Slop Bucket
Spider
Sun-ball
Sweetnin'
Sweetfeed
Tar
Taters
Tote Sack
Tow Sack

Words by Category

Vittles
Wake
Ware
Whitewash
Winder
Witch-water
Witches
Writermarouster

BAG/SACK

Carry Bag
Poke
Tote Sack
Tow Sack

CRITTERS

Boll Weevil
Chiggars
Coon
Coon Dog
Cooter
Critter
Devil's Riding Horse
Guy Scooter-sky
Mosquito Hawk
Polecat
Possum
Redbugs
Snake Doctor
Varmit

ILLEGITIMATE CHILD

Brar Patch Child
Ditch-Edge Child
Wood's Colt

BLANK PAGE

Five

SOUTHERN PHRASES

A BRICK SHY OF A FULL LOAD: Someone who is not quite right in the head.

A GOOD PULL: A long swig of liquor. *Take you a good pull of this shine, son.*

A HEARTBEAT AWAY: Something is very close in proximity or is close to happening.

AIN'T FITTEN TO ROLL WITH A PIG: Not worthy of anyone's company.

AIN'T IT THE TRUTH!: Exclamation.

AIN'T THAT ONE MORE SIGHT: Exclamation of surprise.

ALL BY HIS LONESOME: All by himself. *Billy fixed the bike all by his lonesome.*

ALL FIRED UP: Excited or nervous.

ALL GUSSIED UP: Dressed in finest clothes.

AN ARSONIST'S DAWN: A bright red, Indian Summer dawn.

A PASSEL OF TROUBLE: A lot of trouble.

AS COLD AS A WITCH'S TIT: Very cold, relating either to the weather or to a person's personality.

A REGULAR GO AND COME: A grand party.

A SORRY LOT: A scroungy looking bunch. *Them pup's are a sorry lot.*

AS CRAZY AS A BULLBAT: In late afternoon during the summer the bullbats fly in many patterns chasing the insects.

AS FAIR AS YOUR HAND: Something is easily recognized or in plain view.

AS FINE AS FROG HAIR: Feeling good. *I'm feelin' as fine as frog hair.*

AS FRECKLED AS A GUINEA EGG: Someone with a great many freckles. The guinea egg is completely covered with brown freckled-like spots.

AS HARD AS A LIGHTARD KNOT: A lightard knot is the center of a pine stump containing a concentration of pine pitch. When dry, the stump center is almost metallic in its hardness.

AS LAZY AS UNCLE DEAL: Originated from the extreme indolence of a nineteenth-century North Carolina resident.

AS LAZY AS THE HOUND THAT LEANED AGAINST THE FENCE TO BARK: Self explanatory.

AS LIMBER AS A DISHRAG: A much-used dishrag is very soft and flexible. *She worked so hard she was as limber as a dishrag.*

AS LOST AS A JULY SNOW: Totally out of place, or lost. *A Porsche parked at Bob's Truck Stop would be as lost as a July snow.*

AS MAD AS A WET HEN: Someone who is upset and letting everyone know it. *She was running around yelling, as mad as a wet hen.*

AS MAD AS FIRE: Someone displaying a fiery temper. *He was mad as fire and lookin' for a fight.*

AS MEAN AS A STRIPPED SNAKE: A dangerous person or animal. *Stay away from him, son, he's mean as a stripped snake.*

AS PERT AS A CRICKET: Someone who is feeling in good health.

AS PECULIAR AS MINA MATTHEWS: A local expression originating in North Carolina. According to legend, a drummer visited the area in the latter part of the last century. A woman accompanying him fell in love with one of the men of the area and married him. Her Yankee origin branded her as peculiar.

AS POOR AS JOB'S TURKEY: Indicates extreme poverty.

AS PURE AS THE JEST OF GOD: Virginal. Untouched.

AS ROUGH AS A COB: Corn cobs are extremely rough. The expression comes from rural folk who shelled corn by hand.

AS TOUGH AS WHITELEATHER: Whiteleather is the leather used in harnesses for draft animals and must be very strong. The expression refers to one's attitude or the strength of something. *The steak is as tough as whiteleather. As a lawyer, he's as tough as whiteleather.*

AS UGLY AS HOMEMADE SIN: Someone who is extremely ugly.

AS UGLY AS A MUD DOBBER: A mud dauber is an insect that makes its home in mud cocoons in barns and outbuildings and is very unattractive.

AS UGLY AS A MUD FENCE: Very unattractive.

AS USEFUL AS TITS ON A BOAR HOG: Worthless. The boar is a male hog.

AS WILD AS BURWELL'S BUCK: Legend says that Mr. Burwell of Lillington, North Carolina, owned a cantankerous ox named Buck who frequently escaped, causing havoc. The expression usually refers to young men.

BARKING UP THE WRONG TREE: Heading in the wrong direction. *You're barking up the wrong tree if you think she'll go with you.*

BELLY DEEP TO A TALL DOG: Deep. *The snow was belly deep to a tall dog.*

BELT BUCKLE POLISHING MUSIC: Slow dancing music.

BEST BIB 'N' TUCKER: Best outfit.

BLESS HIS (HER, ITS) HEART: Expression of condolence, sympathy or affection. Generally used by elderly women, but often by younger women who are referring to elderly people, children or pets.

BORN ON THE WRONG SIDE OF THE BLANKET: Illegitimate child.

BOUND AND DETERMINED: Set on something. *She's bound and determined to go to the dance.*

BREAD AND BUTTER LETTER: A letter of thanks.

BROKE AS A CONVICT: Poor. *He held out his empty pockets to show he was broke as a convict.*

CALM AS A DEAD FISH: Quiet, unconcerned. *Zeb's kids could make all sorts of a ruckus and he'd sit there calm as a dead fish.*

CHEW THE RAG: Complain. *Here comes Daisy ready to chew the rag again.*

CLEAN AS A PIN: Very clean.

CLEAN AS A WHISTLE: Very clean and in good working order. *He fixed the car up clean as a whistle.*

COLDER THAN A WELL-DIGGER'S ASS: Self-explanatory.

COME AGAIN?: What? What do you mean? What

was that again?

COME IN AND GET SOT DOWN: Come in and have a few drinks.

COME IN AND SET A SPELL: Sit down and visit a while.

COMMENCE TO: Start, begin. *He commence to tell me as how he could cook better than me.*

CONFIDENCE A STRANGER: To befriend and talk to a stranger.

COON'S AGE: A long time. *Haven't seen you in a coon's age.*

CROOKED AS A DOG'S HIND LEG: Very crooked, sneaky person.

CUT THE MUSTARD: Do the job right. *They went out dancing and he really cut the mustard.*

CUTE AS A BUG'S EAR: Very pretty.

DAGNAB IT!: Exclamation.

DAY LAW!: See definition of "Eh law!"

DEAD AS A DOORNAIL: Definitely dead.

DEAD SET ON: Determined. *He's dead set on*

making it work.

DEVIL'S BEATING HIS WIFE: Term used when it is raining but the sun is shining.

DIDN'T GO TO: Didn't mean to. *I didn't go to break it.*

DINNER ON THE GROUND: Outdoor picnic, usually on the church grounds.

DOG BITE ME!: Exclamation. *Dog bite me if it isn't Billy Joe come to call.*

DOG MY CATS!: Exclamation. *Well, dog my cats, you're lookin' mighty fine.*

DOGGONE IT: Exclamation of surprise or frustration.

DON'T DIFFER: Makes no difference. *I'll have a beer, can or draft, don't differ.*

DON'T GET YOUR DANDER UP: Don't get excited or upset.

DON'T GOT DOO-DAH: Poor. *Don't ask me for money, I don't got doo-dah.*

DON'T GET YOUR PANTIES IN A BUNCH: Calm down and don't get so upset.

DON'T PAY ME NO NEVERMIND: Don't pay any attention to me. *Don't pay me no nevermind, I'll just sit and read.*

DON'T THAT BEAT ALL!: Exclamation of surprise.

DO TELL!: Exclamation of surprise.

DOWNRIGHT KIND OF YOU: That's very nice of you.

DRESSED FIT TO KILL: Dressed and made up to the limit.

DRUNK AS ALL GET OUT: Very enebriated.

DRUNK AS A BICYCLE: Wobbly, unsteady.

DRUNK AS A FIDDLER'S BITCH: Drunk as a fiddler's dog who's been into the drinks the audience members have sent up to the stage.

DRUNK AS A SKUNK: Very inebriated and smelly.

DRUNK AS A SKUNK AT A MOONSHINE STILL: Same as above.

DRUNK AS COOTER BROWN: Inebriated and having a good old time.

DUMB AS DAMMIT: Just plain stupid. *I told him not to skate on thin ice, but he's dumb as dammit.*

DUMB AS AN OX: Again, just plain stupid.

EASY ROW TO HOE: Something that comes easy to someone. *Math is an easy row to hoe for him.*

EH LAW!:   An interjection used in responding to a speaker. It can indicate agreement, puzzlement, encouragement to continue, or melancholy endorsement. For example, one person may say, *"What do you think of the price of cotton?"* and the answer may be, *"Eh law!"* "Eh law!" may also be used in place of "You don't say!" Note: In some areas the expression is "Day law!"

END ALL AND BE ALL: The final or ultimate situation. *This ain't the end all and be all; we're not through talkin' yet.* Also refers to the ultimate in a person or thing. *Ain't she the end all and be all?*

FAIR OFF: Fair weather. *The rain is letting up and it'll fair off soon.*

FAIR TO MIDDLIN':   Fine or as well as can be expected.

FAT'S IN THE FIRE: Trouble is brewing. *The fat's in the fire now and you boy's'll get a lickin' for sure.*

FEELIN' FEATHER-LEGGED: Feeling weak in the knees in love.

FEELIN' LIKE A TURKEY IN YOUNG CORN, HERE TODAY AND SOON GONE: Self-explanatory.

FEELIN' SO LOW HE COULD WALK UNDER A TRUNDLE BED WITH A SILK HAT ON: Self-explanatory.

FIT 'N' FALL IN IT: More than a running fit, a real temper tantrum out of control, when the person having the flare of temper says or does something he later regrets. *She's having a fit 'n fall in it.*

FIT TO BE TIED: Someone who has lost their temper. *He was so upset he was fit to be tied.*

FLAT OUT: Drive "pedal to the metal," as fast as you can. *He flat out drove that truck to the ground.*

FLY-UP-THE-CREEK: A person who changes his mind repeatedly. *He'll never make a decision, he's just a fly-up-the-creek.*

FOLLOW THE SOUTH END OF A NORTH BOUND MULE: To plow a field.

FOOL HEAD OFF: Used with a verb to indicate extreme action. *He laughed his fool head off.*

FOOLIN' AROUND: Wasting time. *Stop foolin' around and get on with your chores.* Also, doing something you shouldn't. *Ole Jake was foolin' around with Betty Sue until his wife caught him.*

FOOT-STOMPIN' GOOD: Something that is so good it makes you want to dance.

FROM KIN-SEE TO CAIN'T SEE: A full day, from dawn to dusk.

GALLIVANTIN' GALOOT WITH THE GOIES: He's a playboy out for a night on the town.

GIT GONE 'N' GIT DONE: Get busy and finish the job.

GIT SHET OF: To get rid of. *The farmer decided to git shet of his old tractor.*

GIVE BACK AS GOOD AS YOU GET: To fight back verbally or physically.

GIVE HOLY HELL: To give a good bawling out. *She gave him Holy Hell when he came tip-toein' in the next mornin'.*

GO AT IT: Get busy. *The wood needs choppin' so go at it, son.*

GOD ALMIGHTY'S OVERCOAT WOULDN'T MAKE HIM A VEST: Description of a very conceited man.

GOING ALL AROUND THE ELEPHANT'S SNOUT TO GET TO THE TAIL: Being long winded, a real clatterbox.

GOING THE WRONG WAY ON A ONE-WAY STREET: Not doing something correctly. Also refers to a person who is not mentally balanced.

GOING TO RAISE HELL AND PUT A CHUNK UNDER IT: "Kick ass." To really cause some trouble.

GOOD LORD WILLIN', AND THE CREEK DON'T RISE: If everything goes well.

GOOD RIDDANCE: It is good to be rid of someone or something.

GOT A GOOD NOTION TO: I think I will do something. *I've got a good notion to call them about this bill.*

GOT A MIND TO: Same as above.

GOT IN THE WIND OF: Discover. *Ernie thought he had a good thing going, betting on the horses, until his wife got in the wind of it.*

GO TO LAW: Go to court. To sue. *I'll go to law and fight this ticket.*

GRAIN OF SENSE: Degree of intelligence. *He ain't got a grain of sense in him.*

90

GREEN AS A GOURD: Not ripe or ready. *That boy's green as a gourd and not up to driving a car yet.*

GRIT IN HIS CRAW: Bold courage. *He was a good soldier with grit in his craw.*

GROUNDHOGGIN' IT: Living in poverty.

GROUNDSQUIRRELIN' IT: Hoarding. Saving.

HAPPY AS A COON IN A ROSHEN EAR PATCH: Someone who's got everything they could want at the moment.

HAPPY AS A LARK: Someone who's very happy and light hearted.

HAPPY AS A DEAD PIG IN SUNSHINE: Someone who's very happy.

HAPPY AS PIGS IN A PEN THAT'S JUST BEEN SLOPPED: Self-explanatory.

HAS A TONGUE THAT JUST WON'T STOP: A gossip.

HATTIE CALLED: A greeting used in place of "How are you?" *Hello. Hattie called. Haven't seen you in a coon's age.*

HAVE MERCY ON ME: Give me a break.

HE COURSED THAT BEE TO THE BEEGUM: He followed the bee to the beehive. In general, to track something to its origin.

HE COULD GNAW AN EAR OF CORN THROUGH A PICKET FENCE: Someone with very buck teeth.

HELL AND HIGH WATER COULDN'T STOP HIM: He is determined to do something and nothing can stop him.

HELL BENT FOR LEATHER: In a real hurry to get somewhere. *He ran out of here all hell bent for leather.*

HE'LL STAND THERE OR GET KILLED, ONE (OR THE OTHER): He's stubborn; won't give in.

HE'LL DIG HIS GRAVE WITH HIS TEETH: He's a liar who'll soon get caught. Also, someone who eats too much.

HE'S ALL HET UP OVER IT: He's ("heated up") angry about it.

HE'S A BROTHER OF THE OLD WILD GOOSE: A wild-natured kid who goes along with the crowd, getting into trouble.

HE'S A HOLLERIN' MASTER: He yells a grat deal.

HE'S GOT A HITCH IN HIS GET-ALONG: He has

a limp. Also means, there is something keeping a person from doing what he wants to do.

HE'S NOT PLAYIN' WITH A FULL DECK: He's not right in the head.

HE'S PAID FOR: His number is up. He's a goner.

HE'S SO MEAN HE'D SHOOT YOU JUST TO WATCH YOU WIGGLE: Self-explanatory.

HE'S TOO SORRY TO HIT A LICK AT A SNAKE: Very lazy. *Don't expect Zeb to help you, he's too sorry to hit a lick at a snake.*

HE LAID IT ON WITH A TROWEL: He embellished his story greatly.

HERE'S LOOKING TO YOU AND TOWARD YOU: A drinking toast.

HE SOT UP TO HER REGULAR: He courted her steadily.

HIDE NOR HAIR: Nothing. *I can't find hide nor hair of that tote sack.*

HIS BREAD AIN'T DONE: He's not right in the head.

HOLD YOUR HORSES: Wait a minute.

HOT DIGGITY DOG!: Great! Terrific!

HOTTER THAN A TWO-DOLLAR PISTOL: Very hot.

HOTTER THAN THE HINGES OF HELL: Very hot. Usually refers to the weather, not a hot object or a hot-tempered person.

HOW'S A BODY TO KNOW?: How was I to know?

HOW Y'ALL: Hello, everyone.

HUNKERED DOWN: Stooped over. *She was all hunkered down, working in the garden.*

HUSH YOUR MOUTH: Be quiet. *Hush your mouth, chile, and mind me.*

I DECLARE: Exclamation.

I DON'T GIVE A BUG'S EAR: I don't care.

I DON'T KNOW BUT WHAT: Think. *I don't know but what I will.*

I DON'T RIGHTLY KNOW: I don't know.

I'D GIVE A WAR PENSION: A decent amount of money. *I'd give a war pension to know what's goin' on out there.*

I'D JUST AS LEAVE: I would like. *I'd just as leave we forget it.*

I'D TAKE IT KINDLY: I'd appreciate it.

IF I'D A KNOWN YOU'S A COMIN', I'D A BAKED A CAKE: Self-explanatory.

IF'N I HADN'T A SEED YOU I WOULDN'T A KNOWED YOU: I didn't recognize you.

IF'N IT'S EVER SO AS YOU CAN COME SEE US: When you get the chance, come for a visit.

IF'N IT WORKS, DON'T FIX IT: Self-explanatory.

IF THAT DON'T BEAT ALL: Isn't that something.

I JUST WON'T HEAR OF IT: Don't argue, my mind is made up. *No, you won't go to a hotel, I just won't hear of it.*

I LIKE TO BRAINED HIM: I almost hit him.

I'LL BE DOGGONED!: Exclamation.

I'LL HAVE YOU KNOW: I want you to know.

I'VE A MIND TO GO: I think I'll go.

I WOULDN'T CHOOSE ANY: I don't care for any. Used in declining an offer of food or beverage.

I WOULDN'T PUT IT PAST HIM: I wouldn't doubt him. *He claims he's going to be mayor and I wouldn't put it past him.*

ILL AS A HORNET: Also, *MAD AS A HORNET.* Very mad or upset.

INDEPENDENT AS A PIG ON ICE: Someone who can't be changed or controlled.

IN FOR A SPELL OF WEATHER: A storm is brewing.

IN THE ALTOGETHER: Nude. *She was swimming in the altogether.*

IT WAS NORATED ROUND: It was told.

IT'S NIGH ON TO: Almost. *It's nigh on to sunset.*

IT'S NO BIG TO DO: It's not a big thing. *It's no big to do, I'm just havin' a few friends over tonight.*

IT PLEASES TO NO END: It gives me a great deal of pleasure.

IT PLEASURED HIM: It gives him pleasure. *It pleasured him to be out riding in the fields.*

JUG OF O-BE-JOYFUL: Jug of moonshine whiskey.

JUST GOES TO SHOW YOU: It was expected.

JUST THE SAME OLE SAME OLE: Everything is the same.

KEROSENE CAT IN HELL WITH GASOLINE DRAWERS ON: Ability. *He has no more chance than a kerosene cat in Hell with gasoline drawers on.*

KICK THE UNADULTERATED SLOP OUT OF HIM: Thoroughly beat him up.

KNOCK DOWN DRAG OUT: A brawl or fight.

LAND O' GOSHEN: Exclamation of surprise.

LATCH KEY'S OUT: The door's always open. *The latch key's out and you're always welcome.*

LAWS-A-ME!: Exclamation.

LAYIN' UP: Resting. *He's layin' up a while.*

LEMME TELL YOU WHAT: Listen here.

LET ALONE: Much less. *I can't afford the car payments, let alone the insurance.*

LET LOOSE AND FLY: Have fun. *I'm going to town to let loose and fly.*

LET OUT: Dismissed. *School let out early so the kids*

could make it home before it snowed.

LET'S GO TO HOUSE: Means "see you later." Does not mean "come by and visit." *It was nice seeing you. Let's go to house.*

LICK AND A PROMISE: Do something in a haphazard or hurried manner. *You didn't clean your room, you just gave it a lick and a promise.*

LIGHT INTO: Tear into, verbally or physically. *Pa lit into Joey somethin' bad when he saw Joey hadn't done his chores.*

LIKE A BANTY ROOSTER WORRYING A BULLDOG: *He kept teasing and picking on the boy like a banty rooster worrying a bulldog.*

LIKE A BASTARD SON AT A FAMILY REUNION: An unwelcome outsider.

LIKE A DEAD DOG: Obviously, not well. *He's been feelin' like a dead dog lately.*

LIKE A HOUSE ON FIRE: Something going (burning) fast. *He lit out of here like a house on fire.*

LIKE A PEA VINE RUNNING THROUGH A CYCLONE FENCE: Something is wound tightly in and around something else. *He wrapped his fingers around the guitar neck like a pea vine running through a cyclone fence.*

LIKE A TWO-DOLLAR MULE: Mules are very stubborn. A two-dollar mule would obviously be very stubborn and not worth having. *He's made up his mind and, like a two-dollar mule, he's not changing it.*

LIKE AS HOW: That. *I hear like as how you ain't goin'.*

LIKE A SHOTGUN BLAST AT MIDNIGHT: Something is very obvious or loud.

LIKE AN OLD TICK GETTIN' FAT OFF A HARD-WORKING DOG: A selfish person, a user.

LIKE CANNONBALLS AT GETTYSBURG: Something is scattered about. *His pitching was terrible; the balls were going everywhere like cannonballs at Gettysburg.*

LIKE COUNTRY BUTTER STIRRED UP IN MOLASSAS: Refers to something or someone very smooth. *His voice was like country butter stirred up in molassas.*

LIKE POPCORN IN A HOPPER: Something is growing or multiplying rapidly. *New houses were going up everywhere like popcorn in a hopper.*

LIKE THE FARMER'S OLE MULE HE JUST DON'T GIVE A DAMN: Someone who just goes about his own business and doesn't care about anything else.

LIT A RAG: Hurry. *He lit a rag for home.*

LOOK A HERE NOW: Wait a minute. Hold on.

LOOSE AS A GOOSE: Drunk. Or, extremely relaxed.

LORDY LORDY!: Exclamation.

MAKE OUT: Hugging and kissing. Also to finish. *Make out your supper, now.*

MAKE YOURSELF PLEASANT: Welcome. Make yourself at home.

MARK MY WORDS: Listen to me. *Mark my words, that boy's gonna go far.*

MERCY ME: Exclamation of surprise or frustration.

MIGHTY SHOUTIN' RIGHT: Darn right. *You're mighty shoutin' right I'm mad.*

MIND YOU: Listen to me. *Mind you, I'm not one to complain.*

MORE'S THE PITY: It's a shame. *Zeb's not coming home from boot camp. More's the pity.*

MY BUT YOU DO CARRY ON: You talk a lot.

NERVOUS AS A SORE-TAILED CAT: Edgy. Can't sit still.

NIGH ON TO: Almost. *It's nigh on to supper time.*

NOACCOUNT TRASH: Low class person; poor, shiftless and lazy.

NO YOU AIN'T!: Expression of astonishment. One person may say, *"I'm getting a new car."* The reply: *"No, you ain't!"*

NOW YOU'VE GONE AND DONE IT: Now you're really in a mess.

OF A MORNING: In the morning. *He likes his coffee of a morning.*

OH, SHOOT!: Exclamation. Darn!

ORNAMENTS OF HIS PROFESSION: Jewelry. *The singer wore a lot of flashy ornaments of his profession.*

OUTTA WHACK: Something is not working right.

PAY (HIM/HER) NO MIND: Don't pay any attention.

PICKED UP: To have gained weight. *I've been dieting all week but somehow I've picked up.*

PITCH A RUNNING FIT: Have a temper tantrum,

yelling, stomping feet, slamming doors and breaking dishes, etc.

PLAIN AS AN OLD SHOE: Description of a homely person.

PLUG NICKLE: Fake nickle. Not worth anything. *I don't give a plug nickle what you say.*

POINT-BLANK TALE TELLER: An outright liar.

POKE FUN: Tease. *Don't poke fun at your sister.*

POWERFUL ASHY: Someone is very angry.

PROMISES DON'T BUTTER NO BREAD: Self-explanatory.

PURTY AS A NEWBORN PUP: Very pretty. Usually refers to a young girl.

PURTY AS A SPECKLED PUP: Very pretty. Usually refers to a young girl.

PUT OFF: Tease. *He put me off somethin fierce.*

PUT ON THE GROUND: To set free. *The judge put him on the ground.*

PUTTIN' ON THE DOG: Putting on airs. *She was puttin' on the dog in her new dress.*

PUT ON THE ROAD: To evict or throw someone or something out. *The banker threatened to put Uncle Walt on the road when he couldn't meet the mortgage payment.*

QUICK AS A CAT: Very agile in movement. Also means smart.

QUIET AS A BIRD WHEN A HAWK FLIES OVER: Very quiet.

RARE BACK: Lean back and prepare to make a move. *He rared back and let out a yell to surprise the burglar.*

RIDING TO HELL IN A HANDCART: Someone is on the way to their own destruction. *He's riding to hell in a handcart with all that drinking and carousing he's been doing.*

RIGHT SMART: A considerable amount. Does not refer to intelligence. *He has right smart money.*

RODE HARD AND PUT AWAY WET: Thoroughly exhausted.

RUN TO STORE: To go shopping.

RUN UP AND BUTT: Frustrated or wasted effort. *He tried to repair the car, but all he did was run up and butt.*

RUST UNBURNISHED: To leave unused.

SCARED AS A DOG SHITTIN' PEACH SEEDS: Self-explanatory.

SHINED UP: Dressed up in your finest.

SHINE IN USE: To be much used, worn in.

SHOOT THE SHIT: Talk or gossip. Also, "Shoot the breeze."

SICKER THAN NO LITTLE: Very sick. *That wild car ride left him sicker than no little.*

SKINNY AS A RED WORM WITH THE SHIT SLUNG OUT OF IT: Self-explanatory.

SLICK AS A BUTTON: Refers to someone who is quite cagey. A con artist.

SLICKED BACK: Dressed up with his hair brushed ("slicked") back.

SLIM AND NONE: Very little. *His chances were slim and none.*

SLIM AS A POKER: Skinny.

SLIP OFF TO: Disappear to. *Now where did he slip off to?*

SLOP THE HOGS: Feed the hogs.

SO GOOD IT'LL MAKE YOUR TEETH SHAKE: Very good. Usually refers to food.

SO GOOD IT'LL MAKE YOUR TONGUE SLAP YOUR EYEBALLS OUT: Very good. Usually refers to food.

SO LOW HE COULD HAVE JUMPED OFF A BRICK AND COMMITTED SUICIDE: Feeling very down and depressed.

SO QUIET YOU COULD HEAR A WORM COUGH: Very quiet.

SO STINGY HE COULD SQUEEZE A NICKEL UNTIL THE BUFFALO HOLLERED: Very tight with money.

SO SWEET SHE COULD CHARM A BEE INTO HER MOUTH: Very sweet.

SON OF A GUN (BITCH):   Expression of surprise or description of a person. *Well, son of a gun, it's good to see you. Hellow, you old son of a gun.*

STAY TILL THE LAST DOG DIES: Stay till the party is completely over.

STOVE UP: Feeling bad, sickly. *He in bed all stove up.*

SUNDAY GO TO MEETIN' CLOTHES: Best outfit. Usually the only complete outfit in a person's wardrobe.

SURE ENOUGH!: For sure. *I sure enough am gonna go!*

SURE AS NOTHIN': For sure. *The boy's headed for no good, sure as nothin'.*

SURE AS SHOOTIN': For sure. *That team's going to win, sure as shootin'.*

SURE AS THE WORLD: For sure. *Sure as the world, that boy's going places.*

SWEETER THAN A MOTHER'S LOVE: Very nice. *Her garden is so well-tended and pretty it is sweeter than a mother's love.*

THAT-A-WAY: That way. *He went that-a-way.*

THAT OLD DOG WON'T HUNT NO MORE: Something will no longer work. *You say you have to stay and work late again, but that old dog won't hunt no more.*

THE SAP'S RISING IN HIM: He's angry and looking for a fight.

THERE'S A DEAD CAT ON THE LINE SOME-

WHERE: If there is static on a phone line, someone is sure to claim *there's a dead cat on the line somewhere.*

THICK AS HOPS: Tightly crowded together. *Cannonballs were flying thick as hops at Gettysburg.*

THIS-A-WAY: This way. *Do it this-a-way.*

THICKER THAN REDNECKS AT A WHITE SOX SALE: Usually refers to a crowd or line of people.

TIE ON THE FEEDBAG: Eat heartily. *He can really tie on the feedbag.*

TIGHT AS DICK'S HATBAND: Stingy. *He won't buy me that new dress because he's tight as Dick's hatband.*

TIGHT AS THE BARK ON A TREE: Someone who is stingy with money, time or affection.

TILL THE LAST PEA'S OUT OF THE DISH: To remain at a party a very long time. *Don't invite the Stokes, they'll stay till the last pea's out of the dish.*

TIRED TO DEATH: Exhausted. *She was tired to death of all his fussin' and fightin'.*

TO FLING A JOE BLIZZARD FIT: Refers to someone displaying irrational behavior. Originated from the fits of temper displayed by a Harnett County,

North Carolina, man named Joe Blizzard.

TOOK DOWN WITH: Became ill with. *He took down with a fever.*

TOOK IN: Started. *School took in late on account of the snow.*

TORE UP: Upset, distraught. *He just got fired and he's all tore up over it.*

TUCKERED OUT: Exhausted. Generally used in expressions of endearment. *Bless his little heart, he's all tuckered out.*

TURN OF WOOD: An armload of firewood.

TURN SERIOUS-LIKE: Become serious. *He was doin' just fine till he read that letter, then he turned serious-like.*

TRUTH TO TELL: To tell the truth. *Truth to tell I don't really want to go.*

TRY IF Y'ALL CAN COME: Try to make it.

UP A CREEK WITHOUT A PADDLE: Getting caught in a tight situation.

UPSIDE THE HEAD: Hitting or slapping someone on the side of the head.

WAIT A MITE: Wait a minute, hold on.

WALKING IN HIGH COTTON: Wealthy, well-off. *She's got a new job and she's walking in high cotton.*

WEAR OUT: Punish. *When I find out which one of you made this mess, I'm gonna wear you out.*

WELCOME AS THE FLOWERS IN MAY: A real pleasure. *Come in. You're as welcome as the flowers in May.*

WELL-A-WELL: Exclamation. *Well-a-well, I do declare!*

WELL, I SWAN: Exclamation. Darn!

WE'RE IN FOR SOME WEATHER: It's going to rain or snow.

WHITE SIDEWALL HAIRCUT: When a barber cuts a man's hair and leaves a band of scalp showing all around his head, exposing his ears, he has a *white sidewall haircut.*

WHOOP-DE-DO: A shindig. *We had a real whoop-de-do last night.*

WHOLE NINE YARDS: Yard goods usually come in nine yard bolts. If someone is going all out for something, he would be going fot the *whole nine yards.*

WIDE PLACE IN THE ROAD: A very small town.

WOBBLY-ASS DRUNK: Very drunk.

WORE OUT: Exhausted, fed up or disgusted. *He was just wore out with the whole affair.*

WORTH A SIGHT MORE THAN I PAID: A bargain.

Y'ALL COME BACK NOW, YOU HEAR: Come again.

Y'HEAR. Expression tacked onto end of sentences. *It's about time y'all came in now, y'hear.*

YOU'VE GOT ANOTHER THINK COMIN': Better reconsider. *If you think I'm falling for that line, you've got another think comin'*

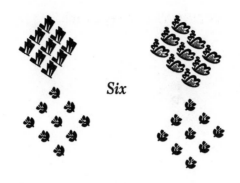

Six

PHRASES BY CATEGORY

WHAT DID HE/SHE LOOK LIKE?

As freckled as a guinea dog

As cute as a bug's ear

As plain as an old shoe

As purty as a newborn pup

As skinny as a red worm with the shit slung out of it

As slim as a poker

As ugly as a mud dobber

As ugly as a mud fence

As ugly as homemade sin

Picked up

Slicked back

He was so buck toothed he could gnaw an ear of corn through a picket fence.

He had a white sidewall haircut.

HOW COLD/HOT IS IT?

As cold as a witch's tit

Colder than a well-digger's ass

Hotter than the hinges of hell

Hotter than a two-dollar pistol

HOW ARE YOU FEELING?

As fine as frog's hair

As limber as a dishrag

As pert as a cricket

Fair to middlin

Feelin' feather-legged

Feelin' like a turkey in young corn, here today and soon gone

Feelin' so low he could walk under a trundle bed with a silk hat on.

Like a dead dog

Rode hard and put away wet

Sicker than no little

Stove up

Tired to death

Tuckered out

Wore out

COME AS YOU ARE

All gussied up

Best bib 'n tucker

Dressed fit to kill

In the altogether

Shined up

Slicked back

Sunday go to meetin' clothes

Wearing the ornaments of your profession

EXCLAMATIONS!

Ain't it the truth!

Ain't that one more sight!

Ain't that the end all and be all!

Bless his (her, its) heart!

Come again?

Dagnab it!

Day law!

Dog bite me!

Dog my cats!

Doggone it!

Don't get your dander up!

Don't get your panties in a bunch!

Don't that beat all!

Do tell!

Eh law!

Good riddance!

Have mercy on me!

Hold your horses!

Hot diggity dog!

I declare!

I don't give a bug's ear!

I'll be doggoned!

Just goes to show you!

Land o' goshen!

Laws-a-me!

Look a here now!

Lordy Lordy!

Mark my words!

Mercy me!

Mighty shoutin' right!

More's the pity!

My but you do carry on!

No you ain't!

Oh, deah me!

Oh, shoot!

Son of a gun (bitch)!

Sure as nothin'!

Sure as shootin'!

Sure as the world!

Sure enough!

Wait a mite!

Well-a-well!

Well, I swan!

WELCOME!

Come in and get sot down.

Come in and set a spell.

Hattie called.

How y'all?

If I'd a known you's a comin', I'd a baked a cake.

If'n it's ever so as you can come see us.

Latch key's out.

Make yourself pleasant.

Stay till the last dog dies.

Try if y'all can come.

You're as welcome as the flowers in May.

Y'all come back now, you hear.

HOW DRUNK IS HE?

As drunk as all get out

As drunk as a fiddler's bitch

As drunk as a skunk

As drunk as a skunk at a moonshine still

As drunk as Cooter Brown

As loose as a goose

Wobbly-ass drunk

HOW SMART IS HE?

Going the wrong way on a one way street

He'll stand there or get killed, one (or the other).

He's not playin' with a full deck

His bread ain't done

WHAT'S HE/SHE LIKE?

A brick shy of a full load

A brother of the old wild goose

A gallivantin' galoot with the goies

Ain't fit to roll with a pig

A hollerin' master

A passel of trouble

A sorry lot

As calm as a dead fish

As crazy as a bullbat

As crooked as a dog's hind leg

As dumb as dammit

As dumb as an ox

As green as a gourd

As lazy as Uncle Deal

As lazy as the hound that leaned against the fence to

bark

As lost as a July snow

As mean as a stripped snake

As nervous as a sore tailed cat

As peculiar as Mina Matthews

As pure as the jest of God

As scared as a dog shittin' peach seeds

As slick as a button

As tough as whiteleather

As useful as tits on a boar hog

As wild as Burwell's buck

God almighty's overcoat wouldn't make him a vest.

Going all around the elephant's snout to get to the tail

Going the wrong way on a one-way street

Got a hitch in his get-along

Got a tongue that just won't stop

Got grit in his craw

He'll dig his grave with his teeth.

He's hell bent for leather.

He's not playin' with a full deck.

He's so mean he'd shoot you just to watch you wiggle.

He's too sorry to hit a lick at a snake.

His bread ain't done.

Independent as a pig on ice

Like a bastard son at a family reunion

Like a two-dollar mule

Like an old tick gettin' fat off a hardworking dog

Like the farmer's ole mule, he just don't give a damn

Noaccount trash

Point-blank tale teller

Puttin' on the dog

Quick as a cat

Riding to Hell in a handcart

So stingy he could squeeze a nickel until the buffalo hollered.

Sweeter than a mother's love

Tight as Dick's hatband

HOW GOOD IS IT?

Foot-stompin' good

So good it'll make your teeth snake.

So good it'll make your teeth slap your eyeballs out.

HOW HAPPY/SAD IS HE/SHE?

As happy as pigs in a pen that's just been slopped

As happy as a coon in a roshen ear patch

As happy as a lark

As happy as a dead pig in sunshine

HOW ANGRY/UPSET IS HE/SHE?

All fired up

All het up over it

Mad as a wet hen

Mad as fire

Fit to be tied

Flingin' a Joe Blizzard fit

Goin' to raise hell and put a chunk under it

Having a fit 'n' fall in it

Hell and high water wouldn't stop him.

Ill as a hornet

Mad as a hornet

Powerful ashy

The sap's rising in him.

WHAT'S HIS/HER FINANCIAL STATUS?

As broke as a convict

Don't got doo-dah

Groundhoggin' it

Walking in high cotton

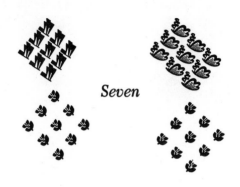

Seven

SOUTHERN NAMES

THE SOUTH IS A MARVELOUS MIXTURE of romance, history and geography. From the pristine sands of the Virginia coast, through treacherous and awesome swamps, rugged mountains and deep gorges, rich fertile farm lands, to the Texas plains, decorated with Spanish moss, magnolia trees and peach blossoms, the beauty of the South can charm the beholder.

The Southerner's love of history and beauty is evident in the choice of place names, names as beautiful, colorful and interesting as the land itself. There are Indian names such as Alabama, Arkansas, Tennessee, Mississippi, Kentucky, Texas, Savannah, Shenandoah, Roanoke, Okefenokee and Chattahoochie. Some names are from our English and European history, such as

Amherst, Sussex, Suffolk, Norfolk, Princess Anne, Raliegh, William and Mary, Southampton, Halifax, Baton Rouge, Rome, Troy, and Athens. There are also funny, even queer, names such as Ripshin Ridge, Possum Quarter, Lickskillet, Kill Devil Hill, Whalebone Inlet, Nine Times, Nowhere Branch, Fair Play, Cat Hollow, Nags Head, Stinking Gut and Smoky Ordinary.

Southerners, on the whole, are a warm, personable, friendly people, with close-knit family ties. This warmth extends to the names they give their children, such as Charity, Grace, Hope, Faith, Felicity and Honey. Most names show a great deal of Anglo-Saxon, Scotch-Irish and German heritage, such as Angus, Cedrenus, Denver, Oscar, Adelaide, Cordelia, Hortensia, Pollyanna and Wilda. Some are biblical, Indian, even botanical names, such as Daisy, Fern, Lilly, Orchid and Rose.

Invariably the Southerner will use the first and middle names together, as in Sue Ellen, Betty Jean, Lilly Mae, Billy Joe or Jim Ed.

Nicknames are especially favored among Southern men, such as Bubba, Buddy, Buster, Cooter, Jeeter, Pratt, Skeeter, Sonny and Junior. Trip is a common nickname used for a man who carries a third generation name such as Wendel James Hayes III.

Southerners are also fond of the use of initials in place of a full name: B.J. (for Billy Joe), R.E. (for Aurelius), and J.R. (for John Robert).

The following is a comprehensive list of Southern personal names.

MALE NAMES

AARON
ABLE
ABRAHAM (ABE)
ABRAM
ADAM
ADAIR
ALDEN
ALFRED (ALFIE)
ALGERNON
ALTON
ALVIN (ALVY)
AMES
AMOS
ANDREW (ANDY)
ANGUS
ARCHIBALD (ARCHIE)
ARGUS
ARLO
ARTHUR
ASHLEY
AURELIUS (R.E.)
AUGUSTUS (AUGIE)
AUSTIN

BARRY
BAXTER
BEAUREGARD (BEAU) OR (BO)
BERTRUM (BERT)
BILLY

BILLY BOB
BILLY JOE (BOOMER)
BOOTHE
BOYD
BOYCE
BRADLEY
BRENTON (BRENT)
BRIAN
BRICE
BRONZELL
BUCKLEY (BUCK)
(BUBBA)
(BUDDY)
BUFORD
BURL
BURNETT
BURTON (BURT)
(BUSTER)
(BUZZ)

CALHOUN (CAL)
CALVIN (CAL)
CAREY
CARL
CARLTON
CARMAN
CARTER
CASEY
CASH
CASS
CEDRENUS
CHESTER (CHET)

CLARENCE
CLAUDE
CLAYTON (CLAY)
CLAUDE
CLEOFUS
CLETUS
CLIFFORD (CLIFF)
CLYDE
CODY
COLEMAN (COLE)
COLLIS
CONNOR
CONWAY (COOTER)
COY
CURTIS (CURT)

DALLAS
DALE
DALTON
DANIEL
DARCY
DARRELL
DAVID
DEACON (DEKE)
DEAN
DELMAN (DEL)
DENVER
DEWEY
DEWITT
DILLON
DORSEY
DOUGLAS (DOUG)

DOYLE
DUDLEY
DURMOND
DWIGHT

EARL
EARNEST
EGBERT
ELDON
ELEM
ELIJAH
ELMER
EMMETT
ENOCH
ERWIN
EZEKIAL (ZEKE)
EZRA

FARLEY
FARON
FARRELL
FELTON
FERLIN
FITZHUGH (FITZ)
FLEMING (FLEM)
FLETCHER (FLETCH)
FLOYD
FRANCIS
FRED

GARFIELD (GAR)
GARNER

GARON
GARVEY
GAVON
GEORGE
GLEN
GILBERT
GOWAN
GRADY
GRAM
GRANT
GREGORY (GREG)

HAMBO (HAM)
HANSON
HAP
HARGUS
HARMON
HAROLD
HEATH
HECTOR (HEC)
HENRY (HANK)
HERBERT (HERB)
HERMAN
HOLLIS
HOMER
HORACE
HORTON
HOUSTON
HOYT
HUBERT

IKE

IRA
ISAAC

JACOB (JAKE)
JACKSON (JACK)
JADIE
JAMISON
JASPER
JASON
(JEETER)
JEREMIAH
JEREMY
JESSE
JETHRO
JIM ED
JIM BOB
JODY
JOE BOB
JOHN BOB
JONAH
JONAS
JUDD
(JUNIOR)
JUSTIN
JUSTUS

KENNETH (KENNY)
KIRKLAND (KIRK)
KYLE

LAFAYETTE
LAMAR

LANDON
LEE
LELAND
LEON
LEONARD (LEN)
LEROY
LESTER
LEWIS (LEW)
LIJAH
LILLARD
LINDSAY
LLOYD
LONNIE
LOUIS (LOU)
LUCIUS
LUKE
LUTHER

MACDONALD (MAC)
MARCUS (MARC)
MARLOW
MARSHALL (MARSH)
MARTIN (MARTY)
MARVEL
MARVIN
MARVIS
MASON
MAXWELL (MAX)
MAYNARD
MELVIN (MEL)
MERLE
MICHAEL (MICKEY)

MILTON (MILT)
MINYARD
MITCHELL (MITCH)
MOE
MORGAN
MORRIS
MOSES (MOSE) or (MOE)
MURRAY

NARVEL
NATHANIEL (NATE) or (NAT)
NATHAN

OBEDIAH (OBIE)
OCIE
ODELL (ODIE)
OLIVER (OLLIE)
OPIE
ORVILLE
OSCAR
OTIS
OWEN

PALMER
PERCY
PORTER
(PRATT)
PRESTON

QUENTIN
QUINCEY

RAIFORD (RAFE)
RAMSEY
RANDALL (RANDY)
RAYFORD
RAYMOND (RAY)
RAZZY
REESE
REXFORD (REX)
RILEY
RONALD (RONNY)
RORY
ROSCOE
ROY
RUPERT
RUSSELL (RUSS)
RYAN

SAMUEL (SAM)
SANDORD (SANDY)
SANBERRY
SAUNDERS
SCHYLER
SEYMOUR
SHANE
SHERMAN
SHERWIN (SKEETER) or (SONNY)

TAD
TANNER
TEMPLE
TODD
TRAVIS (TRIP)

TROY
TYLER
TYREE

VAUGHN
VERNON (VERN)
VICTOR

WADE
WALTER
WARNER
WARREN
WAYLON
WAYMORE
WEBB
WELDON
WENDEL
WESLEY (WES)
WILEY
WILLARD
WILLIAM (WILL)
WOODY
WYNN

YANCEY

ZANE
ZEBEDIAH (ZEB)
ZEKE

FEMALE NAMES

ABIGALE (ABBY)
ADELAIDE
ADELLE
AGIE
ALDOTHA
ALICE
ALMA
AMANDA
AMBER
AMELIA (AMY)
ANNETTE
ANNIE
APRIL
ASHLEY
AUDREY
AUTUMN
AURORA
AVIE

BARBARA (BOBBIE)
BARBARA ANN
BARBARA ELLEN
BEDELIA
BELINDA
BERNICE
BERTHA
BESSIE
BETTY
BETTY ANN

BETTY SUE
BETTY LOU
BEULAH
BILLY JEAN
BIRTIE
BRENDA

CALLIE
CAMILLA
CARLA
CAREEN (CARRIE)
CARRIE LEE
CASSANDRA (CASSIE)
CHARITY
CHARLENE
CHARLOTTE
CHASTITY
CHERISH
CHERISE
CHERRY
CLEMENTINE
COLLEEN
CORA
CORDELIA
CORNELIA
CORY
CRYSTAL

DAISY
DAWN
DEAREST
DELANIA

DELIA
DELENE
DELILAH
DELLA
DEMECIA
DENA
DESSIE
DEMITY
DINAH
DIXIE
DOLLY
DORA
DORIS (DOT)
DULCIE

EDNA
EFFIE
ELIZABETH (BETH)
ELLIE
ELSIE
ELYSE
EMILY
EMMA
EMMYLOU
ERIN
ESALEE
ESTELLE
ESTER
ESTHER
ETHEL
EULA
EUNIVE

EVE
EVA
EXA

FAITH
FAYE
FELICIA
FELICITY
FERN

GERTRUDE
GINGER
GIRTIE
GLADYS
GRACE

HARMONY
HARRIETT
HATTIE
HAZEL
HEATHER
HERMALEE
HILLARY
HONEY
HOPE
HORTENSIA

IDA
ILA
ILAMAE
IRENE

JEANNE
JESSIE
JENNIFER (JENNY)
JEWEL
JODY
JOSEPHINE

KARLA
KATHRYN (KATY) (KITTY)
KELLY

LACY
LALLY
LARUE
LAURA (LAURIE)
LEE ANN
LEILA
LEONA
LESLIE
LEVA
LILLY
(LIZZIE)
LONA
LORENE
LORETTA
LORI
LOUISE (LOU)
LOVEJOY
LUCINDA (LUCY)
LULA
LULU
LURLA

LURLENE

MABLE
MAE
MAGNOLIA
MAIMIE
MAMYE
MARGARET (MAGGIE) (PEGGY)
MARGO
MARJORIE
MARION
MARVIS
MARYBETH
MATHILDA
MAYBELLENE
MAUDE
MAVIS
MAYBELLE
MELANIE
MERRILEE
MELODY
MILDRED (MILLIE)
MINERVA (MINNIE)
MOLLY
MYRA
MYRTLE (MYRT)

NELLIE
NAOMI

OLA
ONA

OPAL
OPHELIA
ORALEE
ORA MAE
ORCHID

PAIGE
PATRICIA (PATSY) (TRISH)
PAULA
PAULINE
PEARL
PENELOPE (PENNY)
PETUNIA (PET)
POLLYANNA (POLLY)

RACHEL
RAINEY
REBA
REBECCA (BECKY)
RITA
ROSE
ROSANNE
RUBY

SARA
SARAH
SAVANNAH
SCARLETT
SELMA
SHANNON
SHARON (SHERRIE)
SHELENE

SOPHIE
STACEY
SUSANNAH
SUEANN
SUELLEN
SUZANNE

TABATHA
TAMALA (TAMMY)
TANYA
TARA
TAWNYA
THOMASINE (TOMMIE)
TIFFANY

VALERIE
VIOLA
VIOLET
VIRGINIA

WILDA
WILLADEAN (WILLA) (WILLIE)
WILLAMAE (WILLA) (WILLIE)
WILLIE-MAE
WILMA
WYNETTE (WINNIE)
WYNONNA

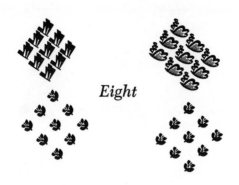

Eight

VITTLES—(SOUTHERN FOODS)

"DOWN ON YOUR KNEES and up with your paws and thank the good Lord for the use of your jaws." You are about to discover the delights of Southern cuisine.

Let's begin at the beginning—breakfast. None of this "Just a cup of coffee, I'll grab a roll at the office" business. Not by a long shot. A real ole-timey Southern breakfast means large slabs of country ham, bacon, sausages, a dish of salt herring roe mashed up in butter, country biscuits as big as your hand, and the never-to-be-forgotten buckwheat cakes, molasses and lots of fresh butter.

Buckwheat cakes and biscuits are the stuff of which dreams are made. These two Southern traditions can raise or ruin a cook's reputation. Biscuits (sometimes called "catheads") must be light, flaky, BIG and smothered in cream gravy. While buckwheat cakes can get a cook run out of town on a rail if they are made from a package mix. True buckwheat cakes are an art, needing careful preparation.

Now that you're properly fortified with a "decent" breakfast, you can face the culinary delights that await you at the midday meal ("dinner" not "lunch") and evening meal ("supper" not "dinner"). These meals might be a "church social," "dinner on the grounds," fish fry or barbecue.

Almost never will you find authentic Southern cooking in a restaurant, unless you dine at a truck stop or travel inland off the interstate highways to an old-fashioned family diner. And then you must be prepared for grease. The South is in the hard lard and heavy gravy belt.

The most famous Southern fish is the catfish—always breaded, fried and served with hush puppies (corn pones made with corn meal and onions and fried in the same fat as the fish). The principal and most plentiful meat is pork in all forms (Southern cured hams are world-famous). Then there are ducks, geese, turkeys and the epicurean delight, "Southern fried chicken."

If you travel far enough into the country you'll also find rabbit, squirrel and opossum. With the opossum (or 'possum) you either love it or violently dislike it. The opossum is a nocturnal animal with a reputation for frequenting graveyards. People with strong imaginations won't come near 'possum and sweet 'taters. On the other hand, the 'possum is juicy and tender, although fat like pork, and many people consider it a treat.

These same 'possum eaters are likely to enjoy chitlins. Chitlins are hog intestines and cooking them can smell up a house to about the same degree as a skunk. Most chitlins are boiled, then fried, and it takes a hardy and hungry soul to eat them.

If you should be lucky enough to attend a real Southern barbecue, or, even better, a barbecue "cook off," you may find yourself in a "barbecue coma." Some people can never get enough, especially if they are eating barbecued pork, roasted properly in a deep pit over hickory wood and basted with the cook's prize-winning sauce. Of course, if you are in Texas, there is nothing as mouth-watering as a side of beef slowly turning on a spit over a charcoal or wood fire with the smell of barbecue sauce filling the air.

To accompany a real Southern dinner or supper, you will be served a variety of vegetables; one is never enough. More than likely these will be: yams or sweet potatoes, spinach, turnips, turnip greens or collards, okra, tomatoes, corn, green beans or black-eyed peas.

No Southern meal is complete without bread, usually in the form of biscuits, cornbread, corn pone, muffins, spoon bread or popovers.

Now, as to desserts. The South is famous for its pecan pie, sweet potato pie, lime pie, peach pie, pound cake, sponge cake, gingerbread and praline candy, to name only a few delectables.

As far as liquid refreshment goes, you will be offered milk, buttermilk, lemonade or iced tea. For more "liberating" refreshment, there is beer, all varieties of liquor (including moonshine) and the world-famous mint julep, a drink made of crushed ice, fresh mint, sugar and mellow bourbon.

Bon appetit!

APPLEJACK: Apple liquor fermented in a crock.

ASH CAKE: A type of corn cake.

BLACK-EYED PEAS: Also "cowpea." Related to the
   bean. Usually stored dry, then soaked and boiled. It
   is a New Year's tradition to serve black-eyed peas—
   for good luck.

BRUNSWICK STEW: A stew made of practically
   everything on the farm and in the woods, including
   chicken, beef, veal, squirrels, okra, beans, corn,
   potatoes, tomatoes, celery, butter-beans, vinegar,
   catsup, sugar, mustard and enough red peppers to
   bring tears to your eyes.

BUCKWHEAT CAKES: Pancakes made with buckwheat flour, potato, water and black molassas, etc. These pancakes are so good it is sacrilegious to add syrup!

CATFISH: River fish—a scavenger, now raised on farms.

CAT HEADS: Biscuits.

CHICKEN 'N' DUMPLINS: Stewed chicken and vegetables with biscuit dough dropped by spoonfuls onto the boiling stew.

CHITLINS: (Chitterlings) Small intestines of hogs. The intestines are scraped and cleaned inside and out, boiled, cut in strips, battered and fried in hot grease. They form a chip, like pork rinds. The hogs are butchered in winter because of the preservative powers of the cold weather. Pieces are cut from the hog and stored in salt then cured in wood smokehouses by slow fires, usually hickory, for many weeks. This becomes smoked ham or pork.

CHOW-CHOW: Pickled green tomato and chili relish.

CLABBER: Curdled milk.

CLING PEACH: Also known as "green peach," "pickle peach" and "yellowstone peach."

COLE SLAW: Shredded cabbage salad.

CORNBREAD: Pan bread made with corn meal. The major bread staple of the South.

CORNMEAL MUSH: Cornmeal cooked in water, served hot as cereal. When cooled and congealed, it is sliced and fried in fat.

CORN PONE: (Hoe Cake) Cornmeal and water formed into a flat patty and fried.

CORN STOCKS: Cornbread made in cornstick pan and baked to resemble an ear of corn.

COWCUMBERS: Cucumbers.

CORN FRITTERS: Canned or fresh corn mixed in pancake batter and fried as pancakes.

COUNTRY CURED HAM: Well aged, cured, honeyed ham. "As spicy as a woman's tongue, as sweet as her kiss, and as tender as her love."

CRACKLINS: Fried pieces of pork rind from which fat has been cooked out, leaving pieces of bacon.

CROWDER PEAS: Larger than black-eyed peas (beans). Usually stored dry, then boiled.

CRACKLIN' BREAD: Cornbread made with cracklins.

DOODLE SOUP: Homemade chicken noodle soup.

DRYLAND FISH: Cornmeal mush shaped in cakes and fried in same grease as fish to give fish flavor.

EGGBREAD: Bread pudding.

FATBACK: Strip of fat from back of hog carcass, usually dried and salted.

FRIED GREEN TOMATOES: Sliced and breaded in seasoned flour, then fried in butter or grease.

FRIED PIE: Pie dough filled with fruit or meat, folded in a triangle, sealed, then fried. (Also called fold-over pies.)

FRITTERS: Vegetables or fish covered with batter then fried in deep fat.

GIZZARDS: Stomach muscle of a chicken. The chicken eats sand or gravel and this muscle uses that sand to grind seeds. Gizzards are usually breaded and fried.

GOOBERS: Peanuts.

GREENS: Turnip, collard, mustard, kale or spinach greens, usually boiled.

GRITS: Coarsely ground grain. Boiled and served in

place of rice, noodles or potatoes with butter, gravy or molasses.

HICKORY NUT "MILK":   Hickory kernels beaten to a milky pulp, a staple of early settlers and Indians.

HOE CAKE: Corn pone.

HOG JOWL: Jowls of a hog, cooked with black-eyed peas on New Year's Day to bring good luck.

HOMINY: Pure grain shucked corn for grits or boiled.

HUSH PUPPIES: Cornmeal batter mixed with onion and dropped by spoonfuls into hot fish grease, served with fish. Legend has it that a cook at a fish fry threw a handful of cornbread batter into the deep fat the fish had been cooked in, and then yelled, "Hush, puppies!" to quiet the dogs that had gathered around the pot and knew a good thing when they smelled it.

INDIAN CORN: Decorative, colored corn on the cob.

MINT JULEP: A favorite southern drink of mint, crushed ice, sugar and bourbon.

MOLASSES TAFFY: Candy made from sugar cane, ribbon cane or sorghum.

MOON PIE: A round chocolate cake with marshmallow filling, usually eaten with an RC Cola.

162

OKRA: Vegetable, usually boiled or fried.

PEACEMAKER SANDWICH: A loaf of French bread stuffed with fried oysters and butter. New Orleans husbands were said to take it to their wives as a peace offering when they came home late.

PECAN PIE: Pecans and corn syrup, eggs and sugar. A favorite, but very high in calories.

PERSIMMON PUDDING: Custard-like pudding made with wild persimmons.

PICCALILLI: Cabbage, pepper and onion relish.

PO BOY SANDWICH: A New Orleans favorite. Long loaf of French bread hollowed out in compartments which are filled with various meats, chicken salad and sausage. The name came from the story that a generous merchant in the French Market used to give them to little boys who called out to him, "Mistah, please give a po boy a sandwich."

POTATO CAKES: Mashed potato pancakes fried in bacon grease.

PRALINES: Pecan candy.

PORK RINDS: Skin of hog, cleaned, boiled, cut in strips and fried.

POT LIKKER: Broth from boiled turnip greens.

PUMPKINJACK: Pumpkin liquor fermented by adding sugar to large pumpkin, covering and storing for two to three weeks.

PUP'S NOSE: Tail of a chicken or turkey.

RAMP: Wild tuber, onion-like plant that tastes better than it smells. It is thought to have curative powers. School kids will eat ramps just so they will be sent home from school—for smelling so bad!

RED-EYE GRAVY: Gravy made from ham drippings and coffee.

ROSHN EARS: Corn on the cob.

SALT PORK: Fat of pork with some meat, used as a seasoning.

SASSAFRASS TEA: Tea made with boiled sassafrass root.

SCRAPPLE: Corn meal and pork cooked, then cooled and sliced, fried as a sausage.

SHORT'NIN BREAD: Bread made with lots of shortening.

SHUCK BEANS: Any type of bean that has to be shelled.

Vittles—(Southern Foods)

SNAP PEAS: Black-eyed peas not fully matured, snapped in shell, like green beans.

SNAPS: Green beans.

SNOW CREAM: Ice cream made by adding sugar, milk and vanilla to fresh snow.

SORGHUM: Grows in stalks, like corn. The juice is pressed out then cooked to make sorphum syrup. The residue is called "blackstrap molasses" and is very thick and strong tasting.

SPOON BREAD: Cornbread cooked like a soufflé, dipped out by spoon.

SQUIRREL. Usually fried or stewed.

STACK PIE: Layered fruit pie

SWEET BREAD: Cake sweetened with molasses.

SWEET POTATO PIE: Custard pie made with sweet potatoes, like pumpkin pie.

TIPSY CAKE: A sponge cake with custard and wine sauce. Formed part of the traditional feast when the preacher came to dinner.

WATERMELON RINDS: Can be pickled or candied and used as a garnish.

WATERMELON CAKE: The interior is colored pink with rose extract and dotted with black currants or raisins. The outside is pale green icing made from pistachio nuts.

WHITEMEAT: Same as salt pork, fried and eaten as bacon.

YAMS: A variety of sweet potato, baked or candied (boiled with sugar).

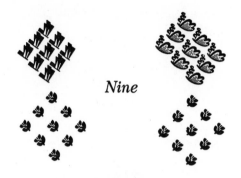

Nine

CAJUN/CREOLE

THE FRENCH POPULATION of Louisiana is divided between the Creoles and the Cajuns.

"Creole" is a term first used in the sixteenth century to describe people of Spanish parentage born in the West Indies. The term later expanded to include descendants of Spanish, Portuguese and French settlers in the West Indies, Latin America and parts of the United States. In Louisiana the term refers to French-speaking people of either French or Spanish descent. French and Spanish-based patois (regional dialects) are known as Creole languages.

"Cajun" is a word referring to the French population who settled in Acadia in Nova Scotia, Canada, in the eighteenth century. They were driven out of Canada by the British and settled in Louisiana. These Cajuns were farmers and backwoodsmen and took well to the Mississippi Delta land.

Cajuns are proud of their distinctive and unique foods. Cajun recipes are very old, French, hearty, country recipes using many wild herbs, spices and peppers.

Creole cooking is quite sophisticated and is a mixture of French, Spanish, Italian and African recipes from all the nationalities that have, in turn, occupied New Orleans. Most of the New Orleans "French Quarter" restaurants serve Creole rather than Cajun dishes.

There are some distinctive grammatical changes that should be noted in the Cajun/Creole speech.

1. The present tense is used in place of the past tense. *SHE WRITE ME MANY LETTER.*

2. *The past tense is formed by adding "been" or "was" to a verb. HE BEEN TRY MAKE ME GO. I WAS WALK HOME.*

3. *"What for" is used in place of "why." WHAT FOR YOU DO THAT?*

4. *"To" is often omitted. I'M GOING SLEEP NOW.*

5. *"One" is often substituted for "a" or "an." SHE ONE FINE WOMAN.*

6. *"Est" is often added to superlatives. HE THE*

BESTEST HORSE.

7. *A very identifying Cajun characteristic is the use of the word "me" at the end of a sentence.* I'M GOING WORK NOW, ME.

8. *Repetition of names and pronouns occurs frequently.* HE ALL TIME TIRED, MY FATHER. HE CALL BILL, BUT BILL, BILL NOT HOME, BILL.

9. *The double negative is frequently used.* I AIN'T GOT NO MORE, ME.

10. *"Don't got" is substituted for "haven't" or "hasn't."* HE DON'T GOT NO JOB.

11. *Most articles, "the," "an," etc., are omitted.* HE PAINT WHOLE ROOM.

12. *Numbers are singular rather than plural.* PHONE RING FIVE TIME.

13. *"Used to couldn't" is frequently used.* I USED TO COULDN'T SWIM, ME.

The most distinguishing factor of the Cajun/Creole dialect is not necessarily the words themselves but the manner in which they are used, as illustrated by the above examples.

The entertainment industry presently has quite a few extremely talented Cajuns in its ranks. In film, independent filmmaker Glen Pitre, a young Cajun writer-producer-director, is almost single-handedly creating a Cajun language narrative film tradition with his films *La Fievra Jaune (Yellow Fever)*, *Huit Piastres et Demie! ($8.50 a Barrel!)"* and the 1986 motion picture, *Belizaire the Cajun.* In music, there are two very well known Cajun performers, Doug Kershaw (the "Louisiana Wildman") whose "Louisiana Man" has become a fiddle standard, and Rockin' Sidney Simien, who in the summer of 1985 had a crossover country-pop hit with a song entitled "My Toot Toot." Also in the entertaining field, Chef Paul Prudhomme's K-Paul's Louisiana Kitchen in New Orleans has been featured on all three networks, BBC and PBS, and his *Chef Paul Prudhomme's Louisiana Kitchen* cookbook is on the national bestseller list.

CREOLE/CAJUN WORDS AND FOODS

ANDOUILLE: Cajun smoked pure pork sausage.

ARMOIRE: Wardrobe cabinet.

BANQUETTE: A paved or wooden walkway, side-walk.

BATTEAU: Flat bottomed boat.

BAYOU: Smal stream. Derivative of Indian word "bayuk."

BOUDIN: A sausage.

BOUILLABAISSE: Seafood chowder made of redfish and red snapper.

CALAS: Rice cakes. Dessert cakes sprinkled with powdered sugar.

COUCHE-COUCHE: Fried cornmeal dough and sugar.

CRAWFISH: Sweet water shellfish, a staple of Cajun cooking.

CUSHAW: Neck pumpkin, cut in squares and baked in skin.

FAIS-DODOS: All night dance party. Literally means go to sleep, also means lullaby.

FILE: Powder prepared from sassafras leaves, an integral ingredient in gumbo, used as flavoring and/ or thickener.

GRITS: Hominy. Is to breakfast what rice is to dinner.

GUMBO: Cajun soup containing a variety of vegetables, meats or seafood and served over rice. Folklore has it that when a Louisianian dies and goes to Heaven and finds there is no gumbo, he comes back.

JAMBALAYA: Highly spiced dish containing rice and meat, pork, fowl or seafood.

173

LAGNIAPPE: A gift or a show of appreciation, a bonus for paying a bill early or buying something in large quantity, etc.

MIRLITON: Green, pear-shaped vegetable.

PIROQUE: A dugout, flat-bottomed canoe, that is paddled or poled through the swamps.

PIQUANT: Very hot jalapeño pepper sauce. This sauce is so popular that there is a Sauce Piquant Festival each year in Raceland, Louisiana.

ROUX: A mixture of flour and oil used to season and thicken Cajun dishes.

TASSO: Highly seasoned Cajun smoked ham.

TOOT TOOT: Sweetheart, or little girl.

ZYDECO: Cajun music that utilizes an accordian.

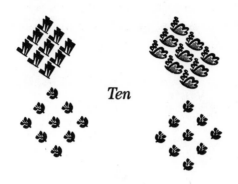

Ten

COUNTRY MUSIC

THE SOUTH HAS ITS OWN brand of music, Country Music (or "America's Music," as it is rapidly being termed). But country music couldn't be contained in the South. It's currently one of the most favored of all musical forms. Country music is to the 80's what middle-of-the-road music was to the 60's and 70's. Its audience has no limits or boundaries—neither in age nor economics. It has expanded into contemporary and pop music formats, movies, television and videos, and has gone international, with country artists now being booked world-wide.

Ask any fan why he likes country music and you'll be told it's the lyrics, the stories that appeal to him and that country vocalists are good singers, having long since left the era of the nasal twang; they give clear, understandable vocal performances. A prime example of country lyric is Charlie Daniels' 1979 Grammy Award winning song, "The Devil Went Down to Georgia." This is the same story that was immortalized in Pulitzer Prize novelist Stephen Vincent Benet's short story, "The Devil and Daniel Webster" (1937), and is also the basis of John Fusco's 1986 motion picture screenplay, *Crossroads*.

In the 1986 radio market research report entitled "What's This Country All About?" compiled for the Academy of Country Music by Landsman-Webster Enterprises, it was discovered that of all radio formats, Country Music ranked #2, second only to Adult Contemporary Radio in the 25–54 age group. Contrary to the stereotypical view that the average country music listener has a modest education, modest income, is a beer drinker, jeans wearer and rural resident, this report proved that the country music audience has 2.3 times more college graduates than All News formats; that the country music audience contains the largest group of homeowner listeners; is ranked #2 in the number of listeners employed full time; and is the third largest group living in central city and metro suburban areas.

In the 1986 Harris Survey on Music, it was shown that 57 percent of the adult Americans polled by the Harris Survey favored country music over rock. Surveys such as the Harris Survey and the above-mentioned Landsman-Webster Report should prove to be a significant factor in determining the type of music to be used in a motion picture or television program aimed primarily for the adult audience.

Music plays an important part in all of our lives and an extremely integral part in any motion picture, television program or musical play. Whether this music is a production number, theme song, background score or source music, it must fit the setting, the action and the mood of the scene. If the music does not enhance, it will conversely detract from, and could destroy, the scene entirely.

Source music must be accurate. If a scene takes place at a truck stop diner in Calera, Alabama, in the year 1950, the producers must be aware of the records most likely to be playing on the jukebox in that diner. The accuracy of the choices of songs could be crucial to the scene.

In this chapter you will find the Top Ten country songs, artists and record labels from 1946 through 1985.

You may wish to have more information about country music than the following list can provide. You might want to know more about the history of country music, the performers themselves, the Grand Ole Opry, Bluegrass music, or a particular producer, writer or musician. There are two major country music organizations, The Academy of Country Music based in Hollywood, California, and the Country Music Association based in Nashville, Tennessee. Both organizations were established for the recognition and promotion of country music and both of their Executive Directors, Bill Boyd (ACM) and Jo Walker-Meador (CMA), are accessible and willing to help. There are also many excellent books on country music. I have found *The Illustrated History of Country Music,* edited by Patrick Carr and published by the Country Music Magazine Press Book (1980), to be extremely thorough.

TOP 10 COUNTRY SONGS

Song Title	Artist	Record Co.
	1946	
1. "New Spanish Two Step"	Bob Wills	Columbia
2. "Guitar Polka"	Al Dexter	Columbia
3. "Divorce Me C.O.D."	Merle Travis	Capitol
4. "Roly-Poly"	Bob Wills	Columbia
5. "Sioux City Sue"	Zeke Manners	RCA Victor
6. Wine, Women and Song"	Al Dexter	Columbia
7. "Someday (You'll Want Me to Want You)"	Elton Britt	RCA Victor
8. "Cincinnati Lou"	Merle Travis	Capitol
9. "Sioux City Sue"	Hoosier Hot Shots	Decca
10. "That's How Much I Love You	Eddy Arnold	RCA Victor

Top 10 Country Songs

Song Title	Artist	Record Co.

1947

1. "Smoke, Smoke, Smoke (That Cigarette)"	Tex Williams	Capitol
2. "It's a Sin"	Eddy Arnold	RCA Victor
3. "So Round, So Firm, So Fully Packed"	Merle Travis	Capitol
4. "What is Life Without Love"	Eddy Arnold	RCA Victor
5. "I'll Hold You In My Heart"	Eddy Arnold	RCA Victor
6. "Timtayshun"	Red Ingle/ Jo Stafford	Capitol
7. "New Jolie Blonde"	Red Foley	Decca
8. "Rainbow at Midnight"	Ernest Tubb	Decca
9. "New Pretty Blonde"	Moon Mullican	King
10. "Divorce Me C.O.D."	Merle Travis	Capitol

1948

1. "Bouquet of Roses"	Eddy Arnold	RCA Victor
2. "Anytime"	Eddy Arnold	RCA Victor
3. "Just a Little Lovin'"	Eddy Arnold	RCA Victor
4. "Texarkana Baby"	Eddy Arnold	RCA Victor
5. "One Has My Name"	Jimmy Wakely	Capitol
6. "Humpty Dumpty Heart"	Hank Thompson	Capitol
7. "Life Gets Tee-Jus Don't It?"	Carson Robison	MGM
8. "Sweeter Than The Flowers"	Moon Mullican	King
9. "Deck of Cards"	T. Texas Tyler	Four Star
10. "My Daddy Is Only A Picture"	Eddy Arnold	RCA Victor

Top 10 Country Songs

Song Title	Artist	Record Co.

1949

1. "Lovesick Blues" — Hank Williams — MGM
2. "Don't Rob Another Man's Castle" — Eddy Arnold — RCA Victor
3. "I'm Throwing Rice" — Eddy Arnold — RCA Victor
4. "Slipping Around" — Margaret Whiting/ Jimmy Wakely — Capitol
5. "Wedding Bells" — Hank Williams — MGM
6. "Candy Kisses" — George Morgan — Columbia
7. "Why Don't You Haul Off" — Wayne Raney — King
8. "Bouquet of Roses" — Eddy Arnold — RCA Victor
9. "I Love You So Much It Hurts" — Jimmy Wakely — Capitol
10. "Tennessee Saturday Night" — Red Foley — Decca

1950

1. "I'm Movin' On" — Hank Snow — RCA Victor
2. "Cattanoogie Shoe-Shine Boy" — Red Foley — Decca
3. "I'll Sail My Ship Alone" — Moon Mullican — King
4. "Why Don't You Love Me?" — Hank Williams — MGM
5. "Long Gone Lonesome Blues" — Hank Williams — MGM
6. "Goodnight, Irene" — Red Foley/ Ernest Tubb — Decca
7. "Cuddle Buggin' Baby" — Eddy Arnold — RCA Victor
8. "(Remember Me) I'm The One" — Stuart Hamblen — Columbia
9. "Birmingham Bounce" — Red Foley — Decca
10. "Lovebug Itch" — Eddy Arnold — RCA Victor

Top 10 Country Songs

1951

	Song Title	Artist	Record Co.
1.	"Cold Cold Heart"	Hank Williams	MGM
2.	"I Want To Be With You Always"	Lefty Frizzell	Columbia
3.	"Always Late"	Lefty Frizzell	Columbia
4.	"Rhumba Boogie"	Hank Snow	RCA Victor
5.	"I Wanna Play House With You"	Eddy Arnold	RCA Victor
6.	"There's Been A Change In Me"	Eddy Arnold	RCA Victor
7.	"Shotgun Boogie"	Tennessee Ernie Ford	Capitol
8.	"Hey, Good Lookin'"	Hank Williams	MGM
9.	"Mom and Dad's Waltz"	Lefty Frizzell	Columbia
10.	"Golden Rocket"	Hank Snow	RCA Victor

	Song Title	*Artist*	*Record Co.*

1952

1.	"Wild Side of Life"	Hank Thompson	Capitol
2.	"Let Old Mother Have Her Way"	Carl Smith	Columbia
3.	"Jambalaya"	Hank Williams	MGM
4.	"It Wasn't God Who Made Honky Tonk Angels"	Kitty Wells	Decca
5.	"Slow Poke"	Pee Wee King	RCA Victor
6.	"Indian Love Call"	Slim Whitman	Imperial
7.	"Wonderin'"	Webb Pierce	Decca
8.	"Don't Just Stand There"	Carl Smith	Columbia
9.	"Almost"	George Morgan	Columbia
10.	"Give Me More, More, More of Your Kisses"	Lefty Frizzell	Columbia

Top 10 Country Songs

Song Title	Artist	Record Co.

1953

1. "Kaw-Liga"	Hank Williams	MGM
2. "Your Cheating Heart"	Hank Williams	MGM
3. "No Help Wanted"	Carlisles	Mercury
4. "Dear John Letter"	Jean Shepard/ Ferlin Huskey	Capitol
5. "Hey Joe"	Carl Smith	Columbia
6. "Mexican Joe"	Jim Reeves	Abbott
7. "I Forgot More Than You'll Ever Know"	Davis Sisters	RCA Victor
8. "It's Been So Long"	Webb Pierce	Decca
9. "Take These Chains From My Heart"	Hank Williams	MGM
10. "Fool Such As I"	Hank Snow	RCA Victor

1954

1. "I Don't Hurt Anymore"	Hank Snow	RCA Victor
2. "One By One"	Kitty Wells/ Red Foley	Decca
3. "Slowly"	Webb Pierce	Decca
4. "Even Tho"	Webb Pierce	Decca
5. "I Really Don't Want to Know"	Eddy Arnold	RCA Victor
6. "More and More"	Webb Pierce	Decca
7. "You Better Not Do That"	Tommy Collins	Capitol
8. "There Stands The Glass"	Webb Pierce	Decca
9. "Rose Marie"	Slim Whitman	Imperial
10. "I'll Be There"	Ray Price	Columbia

Top 10 Country Songs

Song Title	Artist	Record Co.

1. "In The Jailhouse Now"	Webb Pierce	Decca
2. "Making Believe"	Kitty Wells	Decca
3. "I Don't Care"	Webb Pierce	Decca
4. "Loose Talk"	Carl Smith	Columbia
5. "Satisfied Mind"	Porter Wagoner	RCA Victor
6. "Cattle Call"	Eddy Arnold/ Hugo Winterhalter	RCA Victor
7. "Live Fast, Love Hard and Die Young"	Faron Young	Capitol
8. "If You Ain't Lovin'"	Faron Young	Capitol
9. "Yellow Roses"	Hank Snow	RCA Victor
10. "I've Been Thinking"	Eddy Arnold	RCA Victor

1956

1. "Crazy Arms"	Ray Price	Columbia
2. "Heartbreak Hotel"	Elvis Presley	RCA Victor
3. "I Walk The Line"	Johnny Cash	Sun
4. "Blue Suede Shoes"	Carl Perkins	Sun
5. "Searching"	Kitty Wells	Decca
6. "I Want You, I Need You, I Love You"	Elvis Presley	RCA Victor
7. "Don't Be Cruel"	Elvis Presley	RCA Victor
8. "Why Baby Why"	Red Sovine/ Webb Pierce	Decca
9. "I Forgot To Remember To Forget"	Elvis Presley	RCA Victor
10. "Singing The Blues"	Marty Robbins	Columbia

Top 10 Country Songs

	Song Title	Artist	Record Co.

1957

	Song Title	Artist	Record Co.
1.	"Gone"	Ferlin Husky	Capitol
2.	"Fraulein"	Bobby Helms	Decca
3.	"Bye Bye Love"	Everly Brothers	Cadence
4.	"A White Sport Coat"	Marty Robbins	Columbia
5.	"Young Love"	Sonny James	Capitol
6.	"Four Walls"	Jim Reeves	RCA Victor
7.	"There You Go"/"Train of Love"	Johnny Cash	Sun
8.	"Wake Up Little Susie"	Everly Brothers	Cadence
9.	"Gonna Find Me A Bluebird"	Marvin Rainwater	MGM
10.	"Jailhouse Rock"	Elvis Presley	RCA Victor

1958

	Song Title	Artist	Record Co.
1.	"Oh Lonesome Me"/"I Can't Stop Loving You"	Don Gibson	RCA Victor
2.	"Just Married"/"Stairway Of Love"	Marty Robbins	Columbia
3.	"Guess Things Happen That Way"/"Come In Stranger"	Johnny Cash	Sun
4.	"City Lights"/"Invitation To The Blues"	Ray Price	Columbia
5.	"Don't"/"I Beg of You"	Elvis Presley	RCA Victor
6.	"The Ways of a Woman in Love"/"You're the Nearest Thing to Heaven"	Johnny Cash	Sun
7.	"Ballad of a Teenage Queen"	Johnny Cash	Sun
8.	"Send Me The Pillow You Dream On"	Hank Locklin	RCA Victor
9.	"Blue Blue Day"	Don Gibson	RCA Victor
10.	"Alone With You"	Faron Young	Capitol

Top 10 Country Songs

Song Title	Artist	Record Co.

Top 10 Country Songs

Song Title	Artist	Record Co.

1961

1. "I Fall To Pieces"	Patsy Cline	Decca
2. "Foolin' Around"	Buck Owens	Capitol
3. "Window Up Above"	George Jones	Mercury
4. "Tender Years"	George Jones	Mercury
5. "Three Hearts In A Tangle"	Roy Drusky	Decca
6. "Hello Walls"	Faron Young	Capitol
7. "Don't Worry"	Marty Robbins	Columbia
8. "Heartbreak U.S.A."	Kitty Wells	Decca
9. "Sea of Heartbreak"	Don Gibson	RCA Victor
10. "On The Wings Of A Dove"	Ferlin Husky	Capitol

1962

1. "Wolverton Mountain"	Claude King	Columbia
2. "Misery Loves Company"	Porter Wagoner	RCA Victor
3. "She Thinks I Still Care"	George Jones	United Artists
4. "Charlie's Shoes"	Billy Walker	Columbia
5. "Adios Amigo"	Jim Reeves	RCA Victor
6. "A Wound Time Can't Erase"	Stonewall Jackson	Columbia
7. "She's Got You"	Patsy Cline	Decca
8. "Walk On By"	Leroy Van Dyke	Mercury
9. "Trouble's Back In Town"	Wilburn Brothers	Decca
10. "Losing Your Love"	Jim Reeves	RCA Victor

Top 10 Country Songs

Song Title	Artist	Record Co.

lf5w(10P) lf5w(6P) lf5w(5P).

Song Title	Artist	Record Co.

1963

	Song Title	Artist	Record Co.
1.	"Still"	Bill Anderson	Decca
2.	"Act Naturally"	Buck Owens	Capitol
3.	"Ring Of Fire"	Johnny Cash	Columbia
4.	"We Must Have Been Out of Our Minds"	George Jones/ Melba Montgomery	United Artists
5.	"Lonesome 7-7203"	Hawkshaw Hawkins	King
6.	"Talk Back Trembling Lips"	Ernest Ashworth	Hickory
7.	"Abilene"	George Hamilton IV	RCA Victor
8.	"Don't Let Me Cross Over"	Carol Butler	Columbia
9.	"Six Days On The Road"	Dave Dudley	Golden Wing
10.	"You Comb Her Hair"	George Jones	United Artists

1964

	Song Title	Artist	Record Co.
1.	"Dang Me"	Roger Miller	Smash
2.	"Together Again"	Buck Owens	Capitol
3.	"Saginaw, Michigan"	Lefty Frizzell	Columbia
4.	"Once A Day"	Connie Smith	RCA Victor
5.	"Understand Your Man"	Johnny Cash	Columbia
6.	"You're The Only World I Know"	Sonny James	Capitol
7.	"My Heart Skips A Beat"	Buck Owens	Capitol
8.	"I Guess I'm Crazy"	Jim Reeves	RCA Victor
9.	"B.J. The D.J."	Stonewall Jackson	Columbia
10.	"I Don't Care"	Buck Owens	Capitol

Top 10 Country Songs

Song Title	Artist	Record Co.

1965

1. "What's He Doing In My World" — Eddy Arnold — RCA Victor
2. "I've Got A Tiger By The Tail" — Buck Owens — Capitol
3. "Yes, Mr. Peters" — Roy Drusky/ Pricilla Mitchell — Mercury
4. "The Bridge Washed Out" — Warner Mack — Decca
5. "The Other Woman" — Ray Price — Columbia
6. "Then And Only Then" — Connie Smith — RCA Victor
7. "Before You Go" — Buck Owens — Capitol
8. "King Of The Road" — Roger Miller — Smash
9. "You're The Only World I Know" — Sonny James — Capitol
10. "I'll Keep Holding On" — Sonny James — Capitol

1956

1. "Swinging Doors" — Merle Haggard — Capitol
2. "Almost Persuaded" — David Houston — Epic
3. "I Love You Drops" — Bill Anderson — Decca
4. "You Ain't Woman Enough" — Loretta Lynn — Decca
5. "Think Of Me" — Buck Owens — Capitol
6. "Tippy Toeing" — Harden Trio — Columbia
7. "Take Good Care Of Her" — Sonny James — Capitol
8. "Don't Touch Me" — Jeannie Seeley — Monument
9. "Distant Drums" — Jim Reeves — RCA Victor
10. "Would You Hold It Against Me" — Dottie West — RCA Victor

191

Top 10 Country Songs

Song Title	Artist	Record Co.

1967

1. "All The Time"	Jack Greene	Decca
2. "Walk Through This World With Me"	George Jones	Musicor
3. "It's Such A Pretty World Today"	Wynn Stewart	Capitol
4. "I'll Never Find Another You"	Sonny James	Capitol
5. "Where Does the Good Times Go"	Buck Owens	Capitol
6. "I Don't Wanna Play House"	Tammy Wynette	Epic
7. "Your Good Girl's Gonna Go Bad"	Tammy Wynette	Epic
8. "There Goes My Everything"	Jack Greene	Decca
9. "It's The Little Things"	Sonny James	Capitol
10. "My Elusive Dreams"	David Houston/ Tammy Wynette	Epic

1968

1. "Folsom Prison Blues"	Johnny Cash	Columbia
2. "Skip A Rope"	Henson Cargill	Monument
3. "Mamma Tried"	Merle Haggard	Capitol
4. "World Of Our Own"	Sonny James	Capitol
5. "I Wanna Live"	Glen Campbell	Capitol
6. "Only Daddy That'll Walk The Line"	Waylon Jennings	RCA Victor
7. "Heaven Says Hello"	Sonny James	Capitol
8. "Honey"	Bobby Goldsboro	United Artists
9. "Harper Valley PTA"	Jeannie C. Riley	Plantation
10. "Wild Weekend"	Bill Anderson	Decca

Top 10 Country Songs

Song Title	Artist	Record Co.

1969

	Song Title	Artist	Record Co.
1.	"My Life"	Bill Anderson	Decca
2.	"Daddy Sang Bass"	Johnny Cash	Columbia
3.	"I'll Share My World With You"	George Jones	Musicor
4.	"Hungry Eyes"	Merle Haggard & The Strangers	Capitol
5.	"Statue Of A Fool"	Jack Greene	Decca
6.	"(Maggie's At) The Lincoln Park Inn"	Bobby Bare	RCA
7.	"Only The Lonely"	Sonny James	Capitol
8.	"I Love You More Today"	Conway Twitty	Decca
9.	"Darling, You Know I Wouldn't Lie"	Conway Twitty	Decca
10.	"The Ways To Love A Man"	Tammy Wynette	Epic

1970

	Song Title	Artist	Record Co.
1.	"Hello Darlin'"	Conway Twitty	Decca
2.	"For The Good Times"/ "Grazin' In Greener Pastures"	Ray Price	Columbia
3.	"Tennessee Birdwalk"	Jack Blanchard/ Misty Morgan	Wayside
4.	"Don't Keep Me Hangin' On"	Sonny James	Capitol
5.	"Is Anybody Goin' To San Antone?"	Charley Pride	RCA
6.	"Wonder Could I Live There Anymore"	Charley Pride	RCA
7.	"It's Just a Matter of Time"	Sonny James	Capitol
8.	"My Love"	Sonny James	Capitol
9.	"Fightin' Side of Me"	Merle Haggard & The Strangers	Capitol
10.	"He Loves Me All The Way"	Tammy Wynette	Epic

193

Top 10 Country Songs

Song Title	Artist	Record Co.

1. "Easy Loving"	Freddie Hart	Capitol
2. "I Won't Mention It Again"	Ray Price	Columiba
3. "Help Me Make It Through The Night"	Sammi Smith	Mega
4. "The Year That Clayton Delaney Died"	Tom T. Hall	Mercury
5. "When You're Hot You're Hot"	Jerry Reed	RCA
6. "Empty Arms"	Sonny James	Capitol
7. "I'm Just Me"	Charley Pride	RCA
8. "How Can I Unlove You"	Lynn Anderson	Columbia
9. "Good Lovin' (Makes It Right)"	Tammy Wynette	Epic
10. "How Much More Can She Stand"	Conway Twitty	Decca

1972

1. "My Hang Up Is You"	Freddie Hart	Capitol
2. "The Happiest Girl In The Whole U.S.A."	Donna Fargo	Dot
3. "It's Four In The Morning"	Faron Young	Mercury
4. "It's Gonna Take A Little Bit Longer"	Charley Pride	RCA
5. "If You Leave Me Tonight I'll Cry"	Jerry Wallace	Decca
6. "Carolyn"	Merle Haggard & The Strangers	Capitol
7. "Kiss An Angel Good Morning"	Charlie Pride	RCA
8. "Chantilly Lace"/"Think About It Darlin'"	Jerry Lee Lewis	Mercury
9. "One's On The Way"	Loretta Lynn	Decca
10. "Woman (Sensous Woman)"	Don Gibson	Hickory

Top 10 Country Songs

Song Title	Artist	Record Co.

1973

	Song Title	Artist	Record Co.
1.	"You've Never Been This Far Before"	Conway Twitty	MCA
2.	"Behind Closed Doors"	Charlie Rich	Epic
3.	"Satin Sheets"	Jeanne Pruett	MCA
4.	"Teddy Bear Song"	Barbara Fairchild	Columbia
5.	"Amanda"	Don Williams	JMI
6.	"You're The Best Thing That's Happened To Me"	Ray Price	Columbia
7.	"Why Me"	Kris Kristofferson	Monument
8.	"Everybody's Had The Blues"	Merle Haggard	Capitol
9.	"She Needs Someone To Hold Her"	Conway Twitty	MCA
10.	"The Lord Knows I'm Drinking"	Cal Smith	MCA

1974

	Song Title	Artist	Record Co.
1.	"There Won't Be Anymore"	Charlie Rich	RCA
2.	"If We Make It Through December"	Merle Haggard	Capitol
3.	"I Love"	Tom T. Hall	Mercury
4.	"The Grand Tour"	George Jones	Epic
5.	"Rub It In"	Billy "Crash" Craddock	ABC
6.	"Jolene"	Dolly Parton	RCA
7.	"Marie Laveau"	Bobby Bare	RCA
8.	"A Very Special Love Song"	Charlie Rich	Epic
9.	"If You Love Me (Let Me Know)"	Olivia Newton-John	MCA
10.	"Another Lonely Song"	Tammy Wynette	Columbia

Top 10 Country Songs

Song Title	Artist	Record Co.

	Song Title	Artist	Record Co.
1.	"Rhinestone Cowboy"	Glen Campbell	Capitol
2.	"Reconsider Me"	Narvel Felts	ABC/DOT
3.	"Blue Eyes Crying In The Rain"	Willie Nelson	Columbia
4.	"Love In The Hot Afternoon"	Gene Watson	Capitol
5.	"Wasted Days and Wasted Nights"	Freddy Fender	ABC/DOT
6.	"Feelin's"	Loretta Lynn/ Conway Twitty	MCA
7.	"It's Time To Pay The Fiddler"	Cal Smith	MCA
8.	"You're My Best Friend"	Don Williams	ABC/DOT
9.	"Wrong Road Again"	Crystal Gayle	United Artists
10.	"Lizzie And The Rainman"	Tanya Tucker	MCA

1976

	Song Title	Artist	Record Co.
1.	"Convoy"	C.W. McCall	MGM
2.	"Good Hearted Woman"	Waylon Jennings/ Willie Nelson	RCA
3.	"The Door Is Always Open"	Dave and Sugar	RCA
4.	"I'll Get Over You"	Crystal Gayle	United Artists
5.	"Teddy Bear"	Red Sovine	Starday
6.	"El Paso City"	Marty Robbins	Columbia
7.	"I'm A Stand By My Woman Man"	Ronnie Milsap	RCA
8.	"I Don't Want To Have To Marry You"	Jim Ed Brown/ Helen Cornelius	RCA
9.	"One Piece At A Time"	Johnny Cash	Columbia
10.	"Stranger"	Johnny Duncan	Columbia

Top 10 Country Songs

Song Title	Artist	Record Co.

1977

1. "Luckenbach, Texas (Back To The Basics Of Love)" — Waylon Jennings — RCA
2. "Don't It Make My Brown Eyes Blue" — Crystal Gayle — United Artists
3. "Lucille" — Kenny Rogers — United Artists
4. "Heaven's Just A Sin Away" — The Kendalls — Ovation
5. "It Was Almost Like A Song" — Ronnie Milsap — RCA
6. "Rolling With The Flow" — Charlie Rich — Epic
7. "She's Pulling Me Back Again" — Mickey Gilley — Playboy
8. "Southern Nights" — Glen Campbell — Capitol
9. "Way Down"/"Pledging My Love" — Elvis Presley — RCA
10. "Whe's Got You" — Loretta Lynn — MCA

1978

1. "Mamas Don't Let Your Babies Grow Up To Be Cowboys" — Waylon Jennings/Willie Nelson — RCA
2. "Here You Come Again" — Dolly Parton — RCA
3. "Only One Love In My Life" — Ronnie Milsap — RCA
4. "I've Always Been Crazy" — Waylon Jennings — RCA
5. "Heartbreaker" — Dolly Parton — RCA
6. "Take This Job and Shove It" — Johnny Paycheck — Epic
7. "Don't Break The Heart That Loves You" — Margo Smith — Warner Bros.
8. "Everytime Two Fools Collide" — Kenny Rogers/Dottie West — United Artists
9. "Do You Know You Are My Sunshine" — Statler Brothers — Mercury
10. "Someone Loves You Honey" — Charlie Pride — RCA

Top 10 Country Songs

Song Title	Artist	Record Co.

1979

1. "I Just Fall In Love Again"	Anne Murray	Capitol
2. "If I Said You Have A Beautiful Body Would You Hold It Against Me?"	Bellamy Brothers	Warner Bros.
3. "Amanda"	Waylon Jennings	RCA
4. "Every Which Way But Loose"	Eddie Rabbitt	Elektra
5. "Golden Tears"	Dave and Sugar	RCA
6. "She Believes In Me"	Kenny Rogers	United Artists
7. "The Gambler"	Kenny Rogers	United Artists
8. "You're The Only One"	Dolly Parton	RCA
9. "Sleeping Single In A Double Bed"	Barbara Mandrell	MCA
10. "Why Have You Left The One You Left Me For"	Crystal Gayle	United Artists

1980

1. "My Heart"/"Silent Night (After The Fight)"	Ronnie Milsap	RCA
2. "One Day At A Time"	Crysty Lane	United Artists
3. "He Stopped Loving Her Today"	George Jones	Epic
4. "Dancin' Cowboys"	Bellamy Brothers	Warner Bros.
5. "Tennessee River"	Alabama	RCA
6. "Bar Room Buddies"	Merle Haggard/ Clint Eastwood	Elektra
7. "True Love Ways"	Mickey Gilley	Epic
8. "Coward of the County"	Kenny Rogers	United Artists
9. "Cowboys and Clowns"	Ronnie Milsap	RCA
10. "Stand By Me"	Mickey Gilley	Asylum

Top 10 Country Songs

Song Title	Artist	Record Co.

1981

	Song Title	Artist	Record Co.
1.	"Fire And Smoke"	Earl Thomas Conley	Sunbird
2.	"There's No Gettin' Over Me"	Ronnie Milsap	RCA
3.	"Seven Year Ache"	Rosanne Cash	Columbia
4.	"I Don't Need You"	Kenny Rogers	Liberty
5.	"Party Time"	T.G. Sheppard	Warner Bros.
6.	"But You Know I Love You"	Dolly Parton	RCA
7.	"Midnight Hauler"/ "Scratch My Back"	Razzy Bailey	RCA
8.	"Friends"	Razzy Bailey	RCA
9.	"Feels So Right"	Alabama	RCA
10.	"Too Many Lovers"	Crystal Gayle	Columbia

1982

	Song Title	Artist	Record Co.
1.	"Always On My Mind"	Willie Nelson	Columbia
2.	"Nobody"	Sylvia	RCA
3.	"What's Forever For"	Michael Murphey	Liberty
4.	"Crying My Heart Out Over You"	Ricky Skaggs	Epic
5.	"I'm Gonna Hire A Wino To Decorate Our Home"	David Frizzell	Warner Bros.
6.	"Just To Satisfy You"	Waylon Jennings/ Willie Nelson	RCA
7.	"She Got The Goldmine (I Got The Shaft)"	Jerry Reed	RCA
8.	"If You're Thinking You Want A Stranger"	George Strait	MCA
9.	"A Country Boy Can Survive"	Hank Williams, Jr.	Elektra
10.	"She Left Love All Over Me"	Razzy Bailey	RCA

Top 10 Country Songs

Song Title	Artist	Record Co.

1983

1. "Jose Cuervo" — Shelly West — Warner Bros.
2. "You're Gonna Ruin My Bad Reputation" — Ronnie McDowell — Epic
3. "What Ever Happend To Old Fashioned Love" — B.J. Thomas — Cleveland
4. "He's A Heartache" — Janie Fricke — Columbia
5. "A Fire I Can't Put Out" — George Strait — MCA
6. "Pancho & Lefty" — Willie Nelson/ Merle Haggard — Epic
7. "You're The First Time I've Thought About Leaving" — Reba McEntire — Mercury
8. "I'm Only In It For The Love" — John Conlee — MCA
9. "Swingin'" — John Anderson — Warner Bros.
10. "Night Games" — Charley Pride — RCA

1984

1. "When We Make Love" — Alabama — RCA
2. "Roll On" — Alabama — RCA
3. "I Guess It Never Hurts" — Oakridge Boys — MCA
4. "If You're Gonna Play In Texas" — Alabama — RCA
5. "Let's Stop Talkin' About It" — Janie Fricke — Columbia
6. "If The Fall Don't Get You" — Janie Fricke — Columbia
7. "Why, Lady, Why?" — Gary Morris — Warner Bros.
8. "Right Or Wrong" — George Strait — MCA
9. "I Don't Want To Lose Your Love" — Crystal Gayle — Elektra
10. "City of New Orleans" — Willie Nelson — Columbia

Top 10 Country Songs

Song Title	Artist	Record Co.

1985

1. "Baby's Got Her Blue Jeans On" — Mel McDaniel — Capitol
2. "Forgiving You Was Easy" — Willie Nelson — Columbia
3. "Girls Night Out" — Judds — RCA
4. "I'll Never Stop Loving You" — Gary Morris — Warner Bros.
5. "I'm For Love" — Hank Williams, Jr. — Warner Curb
6. "Lost In The Fifties Tonight" — Ronnie Milsap — RCA
7. "Old School" — John Conlee — MCA
8. "Seven Spanish Angels" — Ray Charles/ Willie Nelson — Columbia
9. "She's Single Again" — Janie Fricke — Columbia
10. "There's No Way" — Alabama — RCA

1986

1. "Whoever's In New England" — Reba McEntire — MCA
2. "Always Have, Always Will" — Janie Frickie — Columbia
3. "On The Other Hand" — Randy Travis — Warner Bros.
4. "Rockin' With The Rhythm" — Judds — RCA
5. "Touch Me When We're Dancing" — Alabama — RCA
6. "Cajun Moon" — Ricky Skaggs — Epic
7. "I Don't Mind The Thorns" — Lee Greenwood — MCA
8. "Mind Your Own Business" — Hank Williams, Jr. — Warner Curb
9. "Never Be You" — Rosanne Cash — Columbia
10. "Nobody In His Right Mind Would Have Left Her" — George Strait — MCA

Top 10 Country Songs

Song Title	Artist	Record Co.

1987

1. "80's Ladies"	K.T. Oslin	RCA
2. "Born To Boogie"	Hank Williams, Jr.	Warner Curb
3. "Forever and Ever, Amen"	Randy Travis	Warner Bros.
4. "Love Me Like You Used To"	Tanya Tucker	Capitol
5. "Ocean Front Property"	George Strait	MCA
6. "One Promise Too Late"	Reba McEntire	MCA
7. "Shine, Shine, Shine"	Eddie Raven	RCA
8. "You Haven't Heard The Last Of Me"	Moe Bandy	RCA/Curb
9. "Somebody Lied"	Ricky Van Shelton	CBS
10. "The Right Left Hand"	George Jones	CBS

BIBLIOGRAPHY

Readings in American Dialectology, edited by Harold B. Allen and Gary N. Underwood. Appleton-Century-Crofts, Division of Meredith Corp. (1971).

William T. Polk, *Southern Accent*. William Morrow and Company, (1953).

Lewis and Marguerite Herman, *American Dialects*. Theatre Arts Books (1959).

Louisiana, A Guide to the State, edited by Harry Hansen. Hastings House (1971), from Federal Writers' Program.

Bibliography

Tennessee, A Guide to the State, Hastings House (1939), from Federal Writers' Program.

Richard R. Smith, *Alabama, A Guide to the Deep South,* New York (1941), from Federal Writers' Program.

South Carolina, A Guide to the Palmetto State, Oxford University Press, New York (1941). Writers' Program of South Carolina.

William A. Read, *Louisiana French.* Louisiana State University Studies, (1931).

Charlie Daniesl, *The Devil Went Down to Georgia.* Peachtree Publishers, Ltd. (1985).

Margaret Mitchell, *Gone With the Wind.* The Macmillan Company (1936).

Mark Twain, *The Adventures of Tom Sawyer.* Grosset & Dunlap (1946).

Hank Williams, Jr., *Living Proof,* an autobiography, with Michael Bane. A Dell/James A. Bryans Book (1983).

Loretta Lynn, *Coal Miner's Daughter,* with George Vecsey. Warner Books Edition (1976).

Willadeene Parton, *In the Shadow of a Song.* Bantam Books (1985).

Bibliography

Rita Mae Brown, *Southern Discomfort*. Bantam Books (1983).

William Price Fox, *Chitlin Strut and Other Madrigals*. Peachtree Publishers, Ltd. (1983).

The United States Regional Cook Book, edited by Ruth Berolzheimer. Consolidated Book Publishers, Chicago (1951).

The Victory Cook Book, edited by Ruth Berolzheimer. Consolidated Book Publishers, Chicago (1938).

What's Baking in Aiken, Trinity United Methodist Church. Funcraft Publishing, Inc. (1984).

Country Music 1985 Answer Book, Top Ten Records Since 1946, by Joe Woodburn. Country Music Magazine Press (1983).

Erskine Caldwell, *The Caldwell Caravan*. The World Publishing Company, (1946).

William Faulkner, *Collected Stories of William Faulkner*. Random House, Inc. (1950).

Steve Mitchell, *More How to Speak Southern*. Bantam Books (1980).

Ken Weaver, "Texas Crude" (Texas Slang). *Co-Evolution Quarterly*, Vol. 35, Fall, 1982.

Bibliography

R. Reed, "Revisiting the Southern Mind," *New York Times Magazine*, December 5, 1976.

H.A. Smith, "How to Talk Texian in Tin Easy Lessons," *Smithsonian*, May, 1974.

Paul Prudhomme, *The Blue Ridge*. Oxmoor House, Inc. (1977).

Paul Prudhomme, *Chef Paul Prudhomme's Louisiana Kitchen*. William Morrow and Company, Inc., New York (1985).

The Illustrated History of Country Music, edited by Patrick Carr. Country Music Magazine Press Book (1980).

"What's This Country All About?" Country Music Market Survey by Landsman-Webster Enterprises (1986).

For Reference

Not to be taken from this room